MW01102623

To a Monarch Butterfly

You who go through the day
like a wingèd tiger
burning as you fly
tell me what supernatural life
is painted on your wings
so that after this life
I may see you in my darkness

— HOMERO ARIDJIS

Thanks are due to Sandro Cohen, whose Palabra nueva:
Dos décadas de poesía méxicana *(Premia Editores, 1981)*
led the search for the poets and their books; to my wife,
Angela, for helping to carry them, and to the University of
British Columbia for its Humanities and Social Sciences
grant which supported this anthology project.

CONTENTS

Foreword, VII

FOREWORD

MEXICO MAY APPEAR a tropic beyond immediate reach in the midst of a northern winter, but like these poems migrating north of the 49th parallel from Mexican Spanish into Canadian English, Monarch butterflies travel as far. They undertake an annual odyssey, arriving in Ontario from (among other places) the hill of Altamirano in Contepec, Michuacán. Here, Homero Aridjis, the author of the superscription for this volume, was born of a Greek immigrant father and Mexican mother. Herein lies that other nexus that Mexicans, Canadians, and all those in the Americas share: the mixed genes, the migrations, histories and languages of the old and new worlds.

The poets selected here differ in age, origin and style. They are divided into three generations over the twenty-one year spread of birthdates from 1934 to 1955. The late Octavio Paz, Mexico's best known poet and Nobel prizewinner, is a major influence on all. Since his works are readily available, this volume seeks to bring to the reader's attention those other, not-so-well-known influences such as Homero Aridjis, José Emilio Pacheco and Gabriel Zaid.

Zaid has brought wit and humour in Mexican poetry to a fine pitch: smile at a line from a younger Mexican poet and you are most likely being amused in ways that Zaid patented decades ago in his book, *Questionnaire*. Homero Aridjis, with his environmental activism and his *Mirándola dormir*—a love poem as rich as the Song of Solomon, can be heard protesting or singing through the sensualities of a poet such as Carmen Boullosa in the next generation. José Emilio Pacheco ("the Dr. Pangloss in reverse" of Mexican poetry, as Octavio Paz calls him), with his ironic vision, his innovative forms and techniques, has had as large an influence on his younger contemporaries as Voltaire's philosophy and tragicomic *Candide* had on his.

Poems, in any tongue, are not only made up of words and philosophies, but music and effects. These translations should bring the melody of their meaning, small syllable music, and images clearly across the distance monarchs fly. They are chosen to capture "the immediacies of the tropical," which Verónica Volkow refers to in the final poem of this volume, and provide direct sensory satisfaction for the general reader, who wishes to experience the full effects of the verses in English first hand.

In the things, animals, people and places that animate poetry, thoughts come alive and move in visible ways. To miss the visible (live and in musical motion with the verses) is to lose the fullness of the vision. Poetic sense translates as immediately into the five physical senses as music into the universal language of the ear. This anthology picks poems whose meanings are ripe with the shared vocabulary of the senses and which fulfill the tangible mystery of poetry that Victor Manuel Mendiola identifies in his "Poetics:"

It is the song of the unknown
soon become a vision.
The eye moving, bilingual, in through the mouth.

Finally, a unilingual anthology, in removing the language game with two texts, leaves the reader to judge the merits of the English version as a poem in its own right. It avoids being used as a crib to assist readers dealing with the difficulties of the Spanish in the original text. This is not to deny the original or that checking accuracies and attempting alternative renditions is a lively and rewarding activity which translators, language learners and Hispanic poetry aficionados should undertake. Certainly, the translators represented here have all relished it through their involvement with Literary Translation at UBC's Creative Writing unit.

To this end, readers can connect to the website (www.arts. ubc.ca/crwr/monarchs) for this volume, which provides sample poems in the original Spanish from each of the poets and an opportunity for e-mail response.

— *George McWhirter*

GABRIEL ZAID (1934 -)

The thousand and one nights

After the movie, after midnight,
with a peculiar grogginess, I listen
to the ticking-over of my car, afraid I might
just be listening to my own loneliness. Then

a tune, an intoxicating tune,
snaking through the dead of night
skyward, the zig zags want to zoom,
but God gave no car the gift of flight;

the rivers, trees
exotic fruits of glazed amber,
of jade, of ruby

in the dark of the forbidden garden
are saying no,
saying yes please.

A furious clarity

We accept no givens; from here on, illusion.
The light of my eye: a world away, but mine.

Whether you're present or not, the present is given.
At times light rains down, our daily bread.

Thoughts are given you, yours like the birds.
Solitude is given you, yours like your shadow.
Black light shuddering at the thump of day.

Dry-spell

Solitude as thirsty
and opaque
as a summer alone.

Distantly, the next-door neighbour
walks across the planet,
half-asleep.

Save us,
Our Lady of Tears,
through your transparency.

A hunting song

I am not the wind or the sail,
only the rudder that cuts the trail.

I am not the water or the rudder:
one who sings the song, no other.

I am not the voice or the throat
only the song sung by the boat.

Who I am and what I say I do not know,
only where you go I follow.

Havoc

A lion of a sun released, wild
beast, to roar in the doorways.
The uneasiness of the siesta

with not a soul in the square.

The shadows of a bad dream
as rooted as the trees,
wanting to flee, or scream,
but powerless to pull loose.

At the mostmarxistmill

To have to do
is a lot of have-to:
it chains you.

And to not have to
is to own the perfect view
of how useless it is to be you.

Practice mortal

Raise the oars and float
with your eyes shut.
Open them to discover you are
alive: the miracle, repeated.

Get up and walk,
forget this mysterious shore
where you have come aground.

Maidenform

Thoughtful little boat,
leaning over her bed,
moored to the shore
of sleep.

She dreams that she has cast off,
is under full sail,
that the wind is unloosed,
that these are lives she unfastens.

Nudist colony

You need a thick skin
to walk about like a rhinoceros
while the sad giraffes pass by
in their necklaces of pearls.

Or a hippopotamus's enamel
for this enormous brushing of teeth
while the herons come, careful
of their high heels, reeking
like the river through the stones.

To heck with promiscuity,
daring cock-a-doodle-doing,
shutting our naked sisters up
in hair net and curlers.

We hunt another animal, another
that won't be kept indoors,
that shies away and excites us:
Freedom, freedom.

Gales

Death carries the world off to its mill.
Cartwheels of sun through thundercloud
made the countryside outlandish,
boded the end of the world.

Margaritas tumbled
through gales of laughter
in your throat.

Your uneven teeth
bared their petals
as you lifted your breasts to the rain.

Overladen, your skirt turned
like a large leaf being spun dry,
like a tree filled with memories
after the rain.

Your hair smelt of hair.

Soaked through, you laughed
while I wanted to take
your white bones, like a guffaw
at the improbable end of the world.

Crows

A caw in a dead language is heard: whaaat-for.
A door slam in the dark: what-for.
You're right: what-for.
A light what-for blows
and there is a drop in temperature.

An overpowering hush
summons the what-fors.
A deadly parapet: what-for.
A bolt of dead silence: what-for.
Slivers of mincemeat: what-for.
An emptied revolver all your what-fors.
The steam off a cup of coffee, black.

Gull

Light as a bird,
nostalgia, moved
by the blue eternity,
lands on the mast.

Heavens, where to rest
the eyes? Abrupt parabola,
the flight collapses after
its brief reading.

Let it not settle here,
high up, let its weight
lift and leave the mast be
with no omen attached.

Shadow

Wings—what for,
if they rove.

Eyes—what for,
if they evade.

You go with me—what for,
if sick to death of you,
you sic yourself on me.

Temple

And day, ruin enough,
can barely support
such an august light
on its columns.

And in the air the dark
of night, too, pecks
at an eternity overcome
by voracious birds.

And what will be made of
the trail I set about leaving
you, crumbs of me, poems,
ways to find each other along?

Jungle

I like to stroke the hippopotamus.
Scent the what-is-barely-possible: pheasants.
To lie in wait for your ferocious yawn.
Shoot at your howl in its flight.

I like to give you a finger to nibble on,
a perch for your parrots.
See you meditate, naked
monkey, on your tail, the tree of life.

After the mouth-watering Pleistocene,
the purr of a happy panther.
I relish the gratitude
in the eyes of victory.

Sun clock

An odd time. It is not
the end of the world,
only evening falling.
Reality,
the Tower of Pisa
ringing out the hour even
as it falls.

Traffic light

Like caged suns
waiting until—until what?
Like seeing yourself out of the car,
out of the body, out where?
Like bodies driven over
the abyss of who-are-you?

Who are you?

Ipanema

The sea insists on glittering like an automobile.
Between automobiles the sun breaks through.
The breeze races like an automobile.

And suddenly, gloriously, out of the sea,
dripping foam, giggles, nakednesses,
spurts an automobile.

Theophanies

Give up looking; there are no taxis.

You think one is about to arrive, you step forward,
back; you agonize,
you despair.

                        Accept it
finally, there are no taxis.

Archaeologists have made discoveries
of people who died hunting for taxis,
but no taxis.

                They say
Elijah took off in a taxicab, once,
but never returned to tell the tale.

A eulogy on the usual

How we love the usual!
Running into the usual.
Going over it as usual.

How tasty the usual is!
Losing yourself in the usual.
Finding yourself in the usual.

Oh, the ineluctable usual.
Always give us the usual.

Screen sheet shroud

Connectedly,
as if they scarcely move
in the slow bed.

Through the tricky manoeuvres,
each one trying to find
their balance in the dream,

mad, in love,
grotesque, elegant,
tightfistedly, they search

each other blindly,
embrace, separate. Pass-
o doble toward death.

Nocturnal transmission

The African jungles, the Nile
flooding its banks, the Greek coastlines,
an imperceptible smile, the cities,
all winnowed into a look, painting, telephoto.

The stealing of fire, the casting out
from paradise, the poetry, the temple
building, battles, the power and the glory:
all whittled into legend, history, teletype.

Night sleeps and only the clock speaks:
transmitting the world, the constellations,
the universal story.

In the ecstatic binary of the tick tock
the universe expands with the slowness
of grass; all passes, sifted into silence.

Fish bowl with lettuce

Down to the roots, in a retrogressive
glide, the green slope of oblivion
slides over leaf, the smoothest skin
of which its infancies circumscribe,
down to the bog at its heart, where it is alive.

The fish swims green and undistorted
but the tangled prisoners
of her slow curvatures are,
through successive circumlocutions, led
until even the dumb water's held enthralled.

Oh fish, to whom we owe
so much and in whose nets stay snared!
The eye bulging as it dared
expect no more for its slow
revelation than the sly blow.

Imminence

Against the furious winds, availing
oneself of the walls, the rails
of habit, to stay up.
Sleep, king of the jungle.

Cruel gusts of lucidity.
Valve, the slam of the heart, a door.
Branches lifted by the tempest: secretaries
in mid-air, down an elevator shaft.

In this limbo-like morgue, in this can
of sirens *à la crème du Barry*: the leer
of a drowned man. Suspended in time,

while no other option lies open.
At the doors to heaven, a clock
struck, calling us to Communion.

Fray Luis

The urgency and what else
submerged in sleep
after these many years? The house dark
on the way to the bathroom. The clarity

of forgotten verses,
fragments of moonlight through the branches,
like a peculiar reunion in the memory,
joined up with the centuries in the window

that wait for me, taking back on the form
of a sonnet reiterated after these many years,

verses sleepwalked across the fret of the branches.

The urgency and whatever else moves the moon,
the memory,
the bladder in the shadows.

Rippled water

In the wellsprings of time,
there is no hurry, no pressure. Out of space
grows space
like a poplar.

Eternity stays where it is,
looking at itself in the mirror.
When, in the end, blissful, blinking,
time is born like an interruption.

Time, the rib of Narcissus,
is a splinter of eternity,
mirror broken into an Echo of an Echo.

Time bursting in as soon as we are out of it.
I love you, breakaway eternity.
Stay on, blissful interruption.

TRANSLATIONS BY GEORGE MCWHIRTER

GABRIEL ZAID WAS BORN IN MONTERREY IN 1934, OF PALESTINIAN CHRISTIAN EXTRACTION. HE HAS A MAJOR INTEREST IN THE POETICS AND POLITICS OF RAMÓN LOPÉZ VELARDE. AN ENGINEER BY PROFESSION, HE IS THE DIRECTOR OF IBCON, A COMPANY WHICH COMPILES LISTS OF INDUSTRIAL MACHINERY AND SUPPLIERS WORLDWIDE. HE SERVED FOR MANY YEARS ON THE EDITORIAL BOARD OF *VUELTA*, MEXICO'S PRE-EMINENT LITERARY MAGAZINE, WHOSE PUBLISHER WAS OCTAVIO PAZ.

THESE POEMS ARE FROM HIS BOOKS **CUESTIONARIO** (FONDO DE CULTURA, MEXICO CITY, 1976), **SONETOS Y CANCIONES** (EDICIONES EL TÚCAN DE VIRGINIA, MEXICO CITY, 1992), AND **RELOJ DE SOL,** WHICH WAS RELEASED SIMULTANEOUSLY BY AVE DE PARAÍSO (MADRID) AND EDITORIAL NORMA (SANTAFÉ DE BOGOTÁ). GABRIEL ZAID'S ESSAYS ON LITERARY CRITICISM, PARTICULARLY ON THE READING AND INTERPRETATION OF POETRY, WERE COLLECTED IN VOLUME 2 OF HIS COMPLETE WORKS BY EL COLEGIO NACIONAL, 1996. **LEER POESÍA/READING POETRY**, FIRST PUBLISHED BY JOAQUÍN MORTÍZ, MEXICO CITY, 1972, IS HIS MOST CELEBRATED BOOK.

GABRIEL ZAID'S MOST RECENT ANALYSES OF MEXICAN POLITICS AND PUBLISHING ARE IN **ADIÓS AL PRI** (1994), AND **LOS DEMASIADOS LIBROS** (OCÉANO, MEXICO CITY, 1996). HE IS ONE OF MEXICO'S MAJOR ANTHOLOGISTS, AND HIS **ASEMBLEA DE POETAS JOVENES/AN ASSEMBLY OF YOUNG POETS** (SIGLO VENTÍUNO EDITORES, MEXICO CITY, 1980) AND **ÓMNIBUS DE POESÍA MEXICANA** (SIGLO VENTÍUNO EDITORES, 1971) SURVEY MEXICAN POETRY FROM PREHISTORY TO THE PRESENT.

HE LIVES WITH HIS WIFE, BASIA, AN ARTIST, IN MEXICO CITY.

JOSÉ EMILIO PACHECO (1939 -)

The octopus

Dark god of the depths,
fern, toadstool, hyacinth,
between the unseen rocks, through the abyss there
in the dawn, against the currents of strong sunlight,
night sinks to the sea floor, and from the cups of its tentacles
the octopus sips in black ink. So sweet and crystalline
this most penumbrous brine of mother water
is to that midnight beauty, if it goes
tacking to and fro. But on the beach, littered
with plastic trash, this carnal jewel of viscous vertigo
trails like a long-limbed gorgon; and now with sticks
/ they're battering / that stranded udder.
Someone has hurled a harpoon, and the octopus
sucks in death
through this fresh suffocation that constitutes its wound.
No blood wells from its lips; night bursts—
pitching the sea into mourning.
And through it slowly, sadly, as the octopus expires
the earth vanishes.

Vowels

> *A black, E white, I red,*
> *O blue, U green: the vowels*
> In homage to Arthur Rimbaud

A peculiar thing happened on the monitor:
the vowels rebelled.

23

On the screen, lighting up,
the white in the background felt black—
speechless, cutting
and soundless consonants—the ruins
of a Semitic alphabet.
A rune perhaps, an Assyrian tablet,
a Mayan glyph,
the new Rosetta Stone waiting
in the electronic sepulchre for its decoder.

Where did they go, where are they, what are they up to,
why do this to me, leave me like a dead tree,
planted speechless
in the ground since the world's beginning?

Those five improvised signs became aware
of the key to their importance.
Because without them
we're but dust and dumb crustacea, the
incomprehensible clack of pebbles.
toppling through a timeless abysm.

Give me back my tongue.

I want to take the slippery eel
of the word in my hands

I plead for clemency from the absentees.
I have been unfair to them,
for they sound so different in the various languages
(and even in my own),
for their five signs not being enough
to represent the multitude of vowels—
their tyrannical democracy,
their insolent, indispensable dictatorship.

The ideographs of Babel sparkle

—embers that burned in the hearth for a thousand years,
a puddle in which there was a stream—
in the dark night of the screen:
a snow field, victory of silence
over a planet of signs.

But something happened: like a river in a thaw
flowers of water break through the floes.
Their roots poke through
the basalt blocks of the pyramids.

The vowels come back from the dead.
And renewed from the descent beyond the grave
are raised up amid the enslavement of the consonants.

And restore at last the words for me.

The immortality of the crab

> —*What are you thinking about?*
> —*Nothing. On the immortality of the crab.*
> *Anonymous*, Mexican Self-Portraits (1855)

Of all the immortalities I believe in
only yours, friend crab.
        People break into your body,
plop you into boiling water,
        flush you out of house and home.
But torture and affliction
make no apparent end of you. No,

not you, poor despicable crab—
brief tenant in this mortal carapace

of your individuality; fleeting creature
of flesh that quails between our teeth, not you—
but the others of your vast species: infinite crab
takes over the strand.

Vainglory or praise in one's own mouth

With some push   and shove   tirelessly
          or without any halt or hurry
I have won a place forever
          a little to the left of zero
Absolute zero   the roundest
          most slippery   insurmountable zero
I acquired a fine place in the other queue
          next to the emigrants expelled
from posterity   And this
          is history

Job 18:2

When will you ever have done with words?
We are asked that
in the Book of Job
by God—or his scribe.

          And we go on refining, wearing out
          a language, already dried up;
tests
—technologically unsound—

to make water gush
from the desert.

On going back to sea

    A shadow
from the steep sea escarpments
    or the undulating stain
of a fish, or bird, or stone.
    Nothing stirs under the sun
as if the sea
    is the stopped heart of all motion.
Ever since water became sea
    and lost the planet
with these same waves it has been appealing
    in a keening, wet-eyed orison
that switches octaves suddenly to rage,
    storm of the tormented.

    This reach of wide water
to me is the whole ocean
    or as if it were
because always I come back to look at it.
    And when I think of sea
this image forms.
    I carry it so deep inside
that its murmur
    I tell you
is like a property of my blood.

    And when I am no longer here
to look at and to love it
    the sea will have dried out into desert
—to this, the vantage of my brittle subjectivity—
    scattered with the spray
when my grey ashes light up for one moment
    and I am once more
an atom in the nothing or the life everlasting
    in the total sea of that undivided ocean.

To Circe, from one of her pigs

*Circe opened the gates to the pigsty and led out my
companions in the shape of nine-year-old pigs.*
— The Odyssey, Book X

From among all the beasts
that battled in my body against my soul
          the pink pig wound up conqueror.

     Circe, sweetheart,
what serenity and peace we learn at last
          being little more than pigs.
          Not to grunt and groan
after anyone's approbation:
          to screech, beseeching no one. You must understand
how foul and fallible I am, and forgive me.

But there is no spell that can excel the thrill
          of rolling hot haunches in the muck:
          you, the hexer; me, the pig.

What sour bliss to be one more in your pen.
The pigsty is your temple, and we—your congregation.

Enjoy, Circe, the passion of your pigs.
Repay in love the stale grovelling of your swine.

What country is this?

*(An homage to Juan Rulfo,
in his own words)*

We have come,
walking since daybreak.

28

The dogs, barking.

Over crevasses, dry riverbeds.
        Neither seed, nor shadow
        of a tree, nor the root
        of any thing.

The peaks and high ranges quenched, as if extinct.

        Things here grow like that.
        Into nothing much
        for us to talk about.

        Here we don't get rain.
        Any drop
        fallen by mistake
        the earth eats up.
        It disappears into its thirst.

Who would want to make a plain this big?
What is a plain this big good for?

        Not a bird,
        not a rabbit,
        not a thing.

Such a lot of land for nothing at all.

        Some shocks of corn,
        a patch or two of hay
        with twisted stalks.

They gave us this matted sod
to sow.

        But we have no water.
Not even enough water in our wells
        to coax a crop.

Earth like a rock quarry that spits back the plough.

     Hardened sod
     nothing moves across.

This is the land they doled out to us,
shadow heated over by the sun.

     It isn't the time of new leaf.
This is the dry, prickly time of thorns.
     Dry dust
like corn chaff winnowed high.

All through the stubble
     we search.
Our slim hopes and lamentations
     scrambled.

We walk in the midnight,
our eyes stunned with sleep
     and the lost idea.

The wind lifts and carries
     the dry soil away.

     In this discoloured hour
when everything looks sizzled and black
     with not a sign of rain,
     our little plot
starts shrivelling.

     It rains a bit,
     sprouting thorns
     along the lanes.

We are hardened clods.
We are the live icons of disaffection.

What land is this
we have come to?
Everybody goes away.
Only lonely women
and the old ones
stay.

Here we lived.
Here we set up our life.
In a dead and alive place.

Now we hear
only the hush of solitudes.

And that does for us.

Here we have no water.
Here we own only the stones.
Here the dead weigh down on us more than the living.
They wear us out.

There, far-off, the peaks are already in shadows.

Dog days
when the August air
blows hot.

Let us know if you hear tell of signs
or if you see a light someplace.

If there is any smell of peace, or alfalfa
like a field of spilled honey.

Tell us if you see the country we deserve,
if there is any hope
to set up against our pains.

In the Republic of Wolves

In the Republic of Wolves
we are taught how to howl.

But no one can tell
if our howling is threat, complaint,
a musical form, incomprehensible
to anyone not a wolf,
defiance, oration, discourse

or solipsistic monologue.

The impugning of a Philistine

The flies play their wingsong.
But my uncouthness and narrow tastes
don't allow me to appreciate their odd harmony,
find pleasure
in these territories of delight
which are pure form, perfect Mozart
to them alone as public and performers.

I'm insensitive to their art.
Before these symphonic flies, I'm a Philistine.
And as my critical weapon,
as a crushing refutation, I raise the paper.

Butterfly

The cat pulls the wings off a butterfly.

With what great effort in the twilight
the larva sculpted its blooming.
The light dressed it faithfully
with beauty in a fashion never-passing-out-of-fashion.

And it came, humanely, to be delivered unto this.

A spider in the Holiday House Hotel[*]

A spider passed by here.
Swift as a will-o'-the-wisp,
a spider, in its scale, tiny as a mite,
the final reduction, almost, to micro-organism.

It got up onto the bed,
read something in the open book
and lifted a line off with its legs.

It—indifferent, spider in a hotel where nobody
knows anything about anyone—knows it all,
and carries its investigations: where?

Into the notorious night
of its twilit domain,
or unscathed silk of its campaign tent,
which our poor, provisional eyes don't see
(although as requisite for the world to exist
as the web).

Girdled in arrogance it goes by again.

Blots out one more line.
Ruins the sense.

The spider is a miniaturization of terror.
Shoo it away if you wish, but don't kill.
Who are you to know what the spider wants to say?

> *Holiday House Hotel is the motel in Malibu where, according to
> Californian legend, John F. Kennedy dated Marilyn Monroe.*

The Greek "Y": Spanish letter for "and"

On the ruined chapel walls
moss flourishes, but not as lushly
as inscriptions: the jungles
of initials, carved with penknives into stone,
that grow, mating with time, thatched over and confused.

Scrawled letters, awkward and malformed.
At times insults and outpourings.
But invariably
the mysterious initials joined
by the Greek "Y" (that copulative
conjunction): like hands joined at the wrists,
like legs locked together, traces
perhaps of couplings
that were, or were not, consummated.
How can anybody tell?

Because the "Y" of the encounter also symbolizes
paths that fork: E.G.
met F.D. & they loved each other.
Were they "happy ever after"?

Obviously not, nor does it matter much.

I maintain: they loved
a week, a year, a half-century,
but at last
life undid the join, or death split them apart
(one out of two with no other alternative).

One night or seven moons, no love life
ends happily (so we learn).

But even separation
won't prevail against what they had together.

Although M.A. may have lost T.H.
and P. lies alone without N.,
there was love and it burned for a little and left
its humble imprint, here between the moss
and this book of stone.

From **The resting place of fire**
(1963-1964)

For Patricia and Mario Vargas Llosa
"Desire not the night, when people are cut off in their place . . ."

Job 36:20

I

1

Nothing alters the disaster: the wealth
of hot blood transfuses the air with its grief.
At the sheer edge, what imminence or frontier
of rising wind already awaits us in the dawn?

With a coarse gasp
                              the air descends, in an
overweening gush comes inconsolably
down, even to the stoniest place for fire
                                    to take.

And sadly, like a leaf into the air, the blaze
struck up contemplates the incendiary thirst
of time, its eve of ruin—as if leaning out
over the sea, the steep stacks of the cities
wavering pale. What a blue peninsula
wobbling through pitch blackness the flame is,
there, plunged into the night.
So pale and haughty nevertheless;
hard-set, yet still serene, as if
                              struck dead.

2

Today I break off the ache where bloodthirsty
reality stretched on and on intact.
I sift out your still splinter, meekness.
I shift closer to what beset me: the slicks
of toxic air, the disembodied paw
that clawed at the guitar;
its tail, smoking at the metal grille
like the oil of black anger,
its animality let loose.
I burn in your afterglow, the humiliation, jointed
through you to the spire of vertigo that matches
these traces of an asp spiralled in the dust
that time tramping on, scattered.
                              And it's sad.

3

I don't give thanks. I redouble, I shock
the foundations of the quake again with this greediness
to dig back over all the old ravage and decay.
And all the acting-up, the myriad fragments,
the diagonal lightning-flashes set off
scar and press the air
into finding the alert layers of fire
bedded in the earth.

4

I stare without comprehending, I search for sense
in these brutal acts,

                      and suddenly
I hear a beating in the depth of space,
eternity dying,

            and I reflect,
I dwell on my own defiance,
happy the dying rain stings the air
and snuffs this minute out.

10

Blood and smoke fuel the fires.
Nothing curtails their brilliance. But the mountains
soften the centuries, absorbing their rhythms,
staggering, slowing them until they are stone
once more,

         testimony

             in mute stone
that here there was nothing,

                that the beings too
like stone

       wore away into wind.

Being of spectral breath, not a moan
or man or woman now, although it feels out a climax,
even though nothing can draw it back.

                        Time is dust.
Only the earth yields up its bitter fruit,
the fierce whirlwind suspends
everything built by being.
                        The flowers sing on
in their idiotic cyclical pride,
intending to be reborn, sacrificing everything
to scent, reverting back to stone.

II

1

Saltpeter, rust, the patina in the descent
of dust as it spills back over things.
What stubborn engine of erosion whittles at the world,
burns out in transit, dulls the daylight
and in the sick night starts up again?

Disaster is born, the fear it breeds:
the ire that etches out our age in fire.
No one is willing to die, everyone wants
more of life, more of this reality.
Only the Emperor of Woe, *him* in authority
beside the green man who agreed, tinkers
in the dust, seeing to it nothing manages to work or last.

You jumping jackal, king of the garbage heaps,
junkman, Lord of Babylon,
saltpeter and rust will be fuel to you.
For as long as we live
you will be the dust driven across the world.

2
(The gift of Heraclitus)

But, mossily, the water
slips across the windowpanes,
ignoring that it alters,
far from anything we dreamed of, everything that is.

And the only rest for fire lies in taking this shape
with full power to transform.
Air afire and the loneliness of fire
at setting off this fire air is.
Fire—the world's lighting-up, its going-out
always (it was ever) lastingly.

Today distant things are brought home
to me again; what was close scatters far:

I am and I am not the man who has waited
a morning in the empty park for you
beside the river that never flows back, where broken
October light entered the grove (never twice,
never once more).
And it was the smell of the sea: a dove,
an arc of salt
burned into the air.

You were, never will be
anything but surf:
the rush of distant spray sweeping in
on my every deed, through all my words (the only
ones I have, never strange yet never, never mine):
sea, purest of water to the fish,
will never slake our human thirst.

3

Not to lift one's eyes and see the wall of earth.
To push away the dusk. To step nearer
the deep of night
where dawn with all its bustle
waits to break.

4

If the light grows,
it fills the shape
cast by your longing glance.

5

Worlds veer back to tear apart. A star
shoots raging by to war, until miraculously
it is shut, shipwrecked in the grass,
all its flying stuff blown out,
as if (like the tail off a bird) a falcon bolt
had snapped the vapour trailing from the star:
so it felt to the buried body
mangled in the embrace of mortal ground.

III

1

Sour reek of sulphur, the sudden green
of water underground.
Under Mexican ground the floodwaters
putrefy already.
The lake swamps us, its quicksands
clamp shut

on
all possible exit.
Dead lake in its casket of stone.
Contradictory sun.

(There were two waters
and in their midst, an island,
a wall before it
so no salt would sour
our sweet lagoon, where the myth
still spreads wing and devours
the brazen serpent, sired
from the ruins of the eagle. Its airborne
body burns, revving up again and again.)

Under the ground of the city the waters gather
thick and putrid green
to scourge the conquered blood.
Our contradiction—oil and water—
cleaves like a twinned god
to the shore, dividing
everything in two:
what we wish to be and what we are.

(Experiment. Dig over
a few metres of ground
and it unearths the lake,
the thirst locked in the mountains,
the saltpeter
that scours away the years.
And this mud—the corpse
of Moctezuma's noble city
sprawled across it.)

And it will swallow up our sinister

palaces of reflections, very faithfully,
loyal to the destruction that sustains it.

Our emblem in the axolotl: it embodies
the dread of being nobody at all, lapped
back into the perpetual night, where the gods
rot under the lake, and their silence
is golden—like the gold of Cuauhtémoc
Cortés dredged up out of his imagination.

                                Open that door
light the light come closer it's already late
it has got so late let's go so very late already
but time enough today or tomorrow
take hands can anybody see it's so dark
please give me your hand
                                 I'll see you

2

All night I watched the fire grow.

3

In these past years the city has changed so
it isn't mine, anymore—the footfalls
echoed away into its vaults, never to step home.

Echoes footsteps memories all wreckage

Footsteps that are no longer there, your presence,
empty memory echoing in vain.
In a place that is no longer here, where you passed,
where I saw you last in the night,
this yesterday that waits for me in the tomorrow,
this future that crept back into history,
this continual today where I am losing you.

Stanzas

High in the air, polishing its naked flight,
a grey dove vanishes from view.
In that instant at the birth of light
the limitless sky shines perfect, true—
atangle, cloud and bird are one, blurred bright
design on the ground below—so you,
in shadow or some mirror,
are my reflection and my contour.

Not the future, nor its unreal presence
keeps us distant, no longer linked:
it is this slow disaster, our existence,
the fullness of things we think
forgotten. Only in sleep, in its remote essence,
desolately we walk as one. Nothing
will draw you back to that burning centre,
onto the stumbling sands of the encounter.

But from first glance on you go, thralled
in that faithful precinct: memory.
You stay there, impossibly alive, stalled
deep in your own glow and so transitory.
Today everything is rekindled to set all
the old words to an old story.
On the far side of this moment now the strand's
washed out where sea rolled shining in to land.

There is only the silence. No poem
will pick up this lament in its cold echo.
That would be to whine away the sorry theme
with words the wind honed hollow.
Here it comes—nameless epitaph, sun-scarred emblem
our yesterday's obliteration, like slow

grey thistledown, homing in: envoy
of all that was and is, out of the void.

The Georgia Strait

The forest facing the sea
       An eagle high up
on the top of a conifer
    It was dusk
On Vancouver Island
    the sun sank

Perhaps it was the Aztlán of the Mexicans

From there seven tribes set out
and one
    founded the Aztec empire

Of Aztlán only certain names remain
      planted along the coast like stones

The eagle was discovered in the bush
      not heraldic
not blazing with light in the dusk
      Decomposing

It preyed on fish
    poisoned by pesticide   garbage
industrial waste

Eagles cruise over Vancouver
      while the people
watch leviathans of iron on the beach

The Aztecs believed that night

upon night the Sun God
died into the form of an eagle
           and journeyed through the Land of the Dead
to reascend the second day
       (fortified with human blood)
like a jaguar into the centre of the sky

The Vancouver Indians live
           on the Musqueam Reserve
where the Fraser River spills fresh water
           from the mountains into the sea
then spreads wing into the long plumage of waves

The Georgia Strait joins and separates
       Aztlán from solid ground
the Aztec paradise which is extinct
       like Tenochtitlán
city at the umbilicus of the moon

On the Musqueam Reserve
           there are three golf courses
The old lords of the earth
           caddie the sports utensils
of sea monsters

The eagle spirals down
           and the jaguar
has it drained the blood of night?

Goodbye, Canada

Smell of wet wood
The beach at morning with its logs
Grey sand which was bled as flame and catastrophe
    from the volcano
Mist garlanding the sun
The musky mountain
Islands and their startled colonies of gulls
The weight of snow which makes visible the fall of time
A glass garden beneath the fires of nocturnal rain
    perhaps
    they will be your blank hole in the memory
    a trunk of withered postcards
    and maps rotting at the seams
Idiotic garbage which steals the breath from existence:
    memory
But your name will bear the face and the shadow
    of that girl I bade goodbye to forever

TRANSLATIONS BY GEORGE McWHIRTER

José Emilio Pacheco was born in Mexico City in 1939, and still lives there with his wife, Cristina, a writer-journalist for *La jornada* and Channel 11 TV. One of his two daughters was born in Toronto while he was teaching at the University of Toronto; he lived in Vancouver from 1968-69, teaching at UBC's Department of Hispanic and Italian Studies. He now divides his time between Mexico City and teaching at the University of Maryland. He is a member of the Mexican Academy of Arts and Letters. His **Selected Poems**, edited by George McWhirter, appeared from New Directions, New York, in 1987. His most recent books of poetry are **Cuidad de la memoria** (Ediciones Era, Mexico City, 1989), which appeared in a translation by David Lauer from City Lights, and **El silencio de la luna** (Ediciones Era, 1994), winner of the José Asunción Premio de Poesía and republished in 1996 by Casa de Poesía Silva/Era. He is also known as a short story writer and his selected stories were published by New Directions, New York, in 1987, under the title **Battles in the Desert**, translations by Katherine Silver. In the foreword to his selections for **Poetas de una generación, 1950-59** (UNAM, Mexico City, 1988), Evodio Escalante made the controversial statement that José Emilio Pacheco was the greatest influence on that generation both thematically and technically. This influence is evidenced by the number of epigraphs derived from his lines. His zoological moralities and meditations are of particular importance.

HOMERO ARIDJIS (1940 -)

Mitla

Mistresses of what is here and left forgotten
the ants spill back
over the still spaces
dragging lumps of life
toward the shadow world

Unperturbed by wind or time
casting no shadow on the sandy ground
the squalid gentlemen of death
are engraved against the horizon
faintly vampire-like on their spread wings

Between the broken crags that one day will cease to be
above the age-old cypress that will topple one day
leaving not the faintest trace of the extinct gods
or their strict priest who grew into the mist
I look upon a sun that is dying

Bound for the other world
the slow shadows glide low
along the sparse trails of Monte Albán
pass through walls and bodies
with their shivering cold

On the cracked platform at the tombside
a shrivelled priest in a fretworked shirt
unleashes his shade into the dust
and with one skinny finger
traces the shape of shattered constellations

An anonymous conquistador
recalls his steps through the new world

I slept on beds of stone.
Or to tell you truly,
I had a serpent of stone for a bolster
in a feather chamber where the image
of death flickered back at me off every wall.

The roof was a puddle of mud.
Earth lay on my face
and my legs went as blue as the sky.
Like a splinter of noon,
a hummingbird flew out to the left of my dream.

In the flint of that night,
my body blended with the gods'.
On my brow I had a gust of blood,
black sandals for outstriding the wind on my feet
and through my hand a slit for spying on mankind.

Drunk on ritual, I dug in the obsidian knife
and tore out the heart from one of the sacred dead.
Swift messengers carried
the flames I kindled from his chest
to the four corners of extinguished space.

In the stained face of the forest goddess—
I saw hidden the heavenly blaze (we all quest for
in books)—in the eyes of that nameless animal
whose everyday form, or tread in whose passing
I would never hear, or know, or imagine.

One day, out of the darkness of myself, I arrived
at a sleeping township

with hoops through my ears and stripes down my face,
the sea, smiling infinitely with light,
cresting in my eyes.

Since then—perhaps—
my life is a bolt of lightning,
clad perhaps
in the ragged shadow
of a man.

Monte Albán

Light fell here.
Here, memory was laid
to rest in the stone, the mud and ashes,
cranium and bone.
Here, the air became a bird,
flight a tree,
hunger man,
the valley a release
and the hill a green rain.
Here, man was restored to clay,
brought home again to silence,
tucked into the night.

The nightmare

"There is a verse (of Shakespeare's) that says:
I met the night mare."
                    J.L. Borges, "The Bad Dream"

The night mare
made them rear up and kiss
the air in a dream.

His flailing hands
gripped she who has
no edge or end.

Inside: she
grew empty,
a wall of ice.

Never, as in that isolated
carnality, was so much sunk
so hard and fast into the one belly.

Who is she? was the question that clung on
staring from the edges of the bed
at the man and woman he had been.

Self-portrait at six years of age

On the window, a pane of glass separated the hills
from my hands.

Beyond the classroom a door lit out
onto a stair that plunged into the town.

Everything wanted into Spanish:

51

the ash tree, the stones, the sparrow, the blue of the sky.

Striped dress and tongueless shoes,
my pencil drew the country schoolmarm.

I learned to read like we learn how to be:
you, me, father, brother, the shadow on the wall.

Portrait of my father with scissors

It rains in Contepec, my father is inside the store,
the scissors in his hand opening into two blades.

When they shut, the scissors pinch at the bolt of cheap cloth,
as if life were being sold by the centimetre.

Is the metre strip on the counter oblivious to what it measures,
or does it mete out, secretly, the sadness in my father—

for shopkeeper and customer appear cut by the same scissor
of limitless, unreasoning sadness.

It rains in Contepec. The stony afternoon comes down the street
to the house where my mother is stewing peaches.

The evening is green that drifts across the hills
and in through the door to the hall, doorway of all delight.

View of Mexico City from Chapultepec, circa 1825

After the rain on this Friday in July,
everything in the valley spills out from the cap
of porphyry rock on Chapultepec.

Drunk on the setting sun, carriageways
of elms and poplars trail into the city
and exit, bathed in the waters of Lake Texcoco.

To the North on the outskirts of Tepeyac, above
and beyond the wet lick of light on the fields,
the shrine of the Virgin appears, brown as earth.

In the deep South (everything South is deep),
the dying sun's purple fingers
touch the icy shoulders of the Sleeping Lady.

There, between the magueys, where the green streets
veer west, a woman is coming on her own
down one I still take day in and day out of devotion.

Along the highway, the aging day makes for San Angel;
the city slithers into the dark
and time swings through the green tresses of the willows.

A hummingbird draws the shape of escape
from the jaws of a yellow Tom,
the landscape purrs with life, the past moves.

Aunt Hermione

My Aunt Hermione's story has always disturbed me.
Astray for a year, according to my father, in Yugoslavia.
Missing, according to my uncle, on the ship
that took her from Smyrna across the Sea of Nowhere.
The survivors confused the routes taken by the dead
with their own
and still don't know which nightmare, which memory is theirs.

I never saw my Aunt Hermione's face,
but it perturbs me to think of her adrift on the confusions of the past,
without it being possible to ask her what took place,
where she was lost, where found again.
Did she drift through a period without calendars
in a sea without waves, on a ship without sides,
in a secret undertaking to escape from those who loved her?

Did she realize that as long as she was alive,
as far as she might sail toward the Land of No Name
the refugee ship must turn about,
that this is the present time, this is this planet?
One day they certainly did find her
but if she found herself again, can anybody tell?
Suffice it to say, one day she stowed away from this world.

In dreams I see my father's grave

In dreams I see my father's grave
among the graves of the Greek fallen in 1922.
But when I wake, I never find it
among the decomposing bodies from 1922.
What I do see are Turks waving their fists, howling after my father

through the nights of 1922.
But quicker than they slit throats, as beyond further
harm as the bones they have just broken,
my father doesn't die at the hands of Turks
slaying the Greeks in 1922. Another death catches up with him:
his man's heart in his chest.

Love poem: Mexico City

In this valley, surrounded by mountains, there is a lake
and in the middle of the lake a city
where an eagle eviscerated a serpent
over this thorny plant on the ground.

One morning bearded men arrived on horseback
and tore down the temples to the gods,
the palaces, the walls, the memorials,
choking off the springs and the canals.

Over that wreckage, the vanquished built
the victors' houses out of those same stones,
raised churches to their God and streets
down which the days poured out of memory.

Centuries after, the masses crushed it once more,
pressing up the hillsides and into the gorges,
channelling off the rivers and felling the trees,
and the city began to die of thirst.

One evening, along a thronging avenue, a woman came my way,
and all of one night and one day
we walked the nameless streets, the scarred neighbourhoods
of the Federal District: Mexico-Tenochtitlán.

In and out of the packed people and jammed cars; through
markets, squares, hotels we came
to know our bodies, turn two bodies
into one.

Then, when she went away, the city was left,
marooned in its own millions,
its dried-up lake; the smog-bound sky,
the unseeable mountains.

Tourist in 1934

in a bed at the Hotel Genève
she asked me about the mountains
that surround Mexico City
      I brooded upon the solitary breasts of her life
      that lift like bland
      beaks at nightfall

she told me that in Volador Market
she bought jewels a hundred years old
at reasonable prices
      I gazed into those eyes
      with no value at all
      a hundred years from now

she asked me about the Salón México
where men dance in hats and overalls
and about the Retiro restaurant
where fans
hurry of a Sunday evening
after the corrida
to tuck into the innards of the dead bulls
      I embraced her in the intimate night of the room
      and danced in the dark
      and ate into her life

she talked to me of strolling in the suburbs
and chatted about the men on horseback
who whistled at her going by in Coyoacán and Churubusco
　　　I felt jealous of what their eyes saw
　　　and what they did not see

finally at dawn we slept
like a single body
without corners without streets
nameless and faceless
hugged by the shadows of the immense land

Fray Gaspar de Carvajal remembers the Amazon

Old and ailing
I have no fear of death—
I have died many times already.
Up the great river I have sailed
and seen the shadows hanging from the light
and the bursts of echoes from that deafening noise
set off by the crash
of waters into the open sea.
From the steamy branches
of the forest masking the shore
I have seen the poisoned arrow shoot
and watched it fall from the sky
like a needle and thread
the sun's rays and the heat.
Under every cot
there is a sleeping skeleton
and wriggling in every stream
a viper of lost memory.
It is harder to be
an old man who gets cold
in the hours before daybreak
feeling his bones ache

in the rainy season
than to search for the source
of the richest river on earth.
Day after day
like all men I have sailed
nowhere
in search of El Dorado
but like them all
I have found only
the last gleam of extreme passion
at this river mouth
which through its triple channels—
hunger, weariness and rage—
pours death.

Helmstedterstrasse 27

for Betty

History's victims (or prehistory's),
those who lived here, their shadows hang on
like the travelling clothes of those who are no more.

There's a knot in the throat at this bare lath,
those ripped away from between these walls, a foot
creaking in out of yesterday through the door.

At times in the night, an elevator with no one
in it goes up one floor farther than air,
or down, to the bottom of what isn't there.

Men frequently are heard on the stairs
coming to pluck us from the arms
of a body, already departed.

The nightmare awakens us
and outside of sleep we dream on
about whatever is slaughtering us inside.

There's no guarantee that fear finishes at death.
It is a touch above the ends of our hair,
a mite below the blood in our heel, it lives
a step ahead of us and time.

Images for stair, ladder and steps

1

If you were to put a mirror
at the bottom of a stair,
it would extend into another
or float on into nothing at all.

2

If you cut one spiralled in smoke, it goes on climbing.
If you break a wooden ladder, it will make two.
Dig a set of steps into the ground; it will lead into the dark,
making it exactly like a man.

3

A ladder mounted hand over hand
rests two feet firmly on the ground
and the violet of the evening is seen through the rungs

4

The worst thing about a stair
is it doesn't see it is a stair.
I know, like some people
who can't tell if they're human.

5

The ladder is ignorant of how many rungs it has.
I'll count them: 1,2,3,4,5,
                          6,7,8,9,10.

Next in line is air.

6

There is noise and motion
 in the world on and off a stair.
Only the stair stands still on the stairs.

7

How many stairs are there
of wood or stone or smoke
that lead nowhere in this world?

8

The stair,
a poem goes up without words,
comes back down.

Poem written on a plane

You will hear sounds,
and hands approaching to offer
the feminine curve of the earth
and the light so often longed for.

You will hear lights
nearer than thought
and silence closer than your own voice
or the sun's rays sinking over the mountain.

You will hear why
the eyes are carried beyond the everyday
while you stare across at them,
and they at you from inside.

You will hear words slip out,
memories they'll listen to you speak of,
that were on the tip of the tongue
and could not be spoken.

You will hear flashbacks.
To you, to him, to her,
to any time or year, only
half-dreaming them.

You will hear your body—
whose being has no shadow,
no thirst—
coming to pick you up at midnight.

You will hear yourself fall.

These are the sleeping conditions

These are the sleeping conditions, or more like my waking,
seeing what is not, doing what's undone,
digging a grave for this lady graven in my heart,
cutting the moments short to slip through a world without walls,
my eyes glued to somebody who isn't there, flipping things
upside down, hoping to fix the way they operate, like buying
real estate with an unreal buck.

These are the sleeping conditions, or more like the waking,
after moving into the spare bedroom where everybody

61

outside in the street knows her bored face peeps in
even in dreams, a methodical woman sells her meat dear
and a fellow with no faith in himself puts on the image
of some idol to butter up
this hunger in him: woman.

These are the sleeping conditions, or more like my waking,
after mislaying memories, after dumping out the memory,
after mixing up traffic signals so the pedestrians—
including your dreamer—march right on and get lost,
after lining up the days wrong, remarking to nobody
in particular:
"After-the-night-before . . . the-day-after-yesterday;"
after every missing thing turns out to be
some handiwork of mine.

These are the sleeping conditions, or more like the waking,
soaring after dreaming, after seeing, after taking some fantasy
figure for real,
after leaping at the meat in the bed or on the plate,
after twisting and turning after love like a screw
that won't thread into anything soft and female,
into any unfamiliar female, but look with what lazy
luxury death turns us on.

These are the sleeping conditions, or more like the waking,
those shadows dreamed onto the wall
that shake off clawing shadows,
dreaming about somebody who dreams of us,
not knowing who is doing the sleeping, who the waking,
if it's me or her, day after tomorrow or yesterday,
or just this aftermath of us
splitting up in a flash of time.

Two poems composed in bronze

I

Not only do languages die
not only is Sulla's bronze head laid open
not only is the Balinese tiger made extinct.

There are private languages perishing
dreams that strain our eyes to breaking
animals of ours that die of irreality in the street.

Not only the cemeteries of ages past
are catacombed with forgotten gods
our deepest love is lardered with lost words.

II

Sulla's head is not this bronze emptied of eyes
or the nose broken by the blow of time,
or the lips torn clean through to the chest.

It isn't that blind look of unrequited rage
that careers across the centuries
or history that gulps itself back.

Gnashing on air
Sulla's head is what men of all times
carry on their shoulders.

Elio Antonio de Nebrija: grammarian at war

A word is a thought pronounced by the mouth.
FR. HORTENSIO FELIX PARAVICINO, *Marial and Santoral*, f. 159
If the word did not come from God time would not obey it.
D. ANTONIO DE MENDOZA, *The Life of Our Lady*

He left behind the land of his birth,
of his childhood years by the Guadalquivir,
to cross over into Italy and reclaim the expatriate Spanish authors
writing in Latin.

He returned to Salamanca and opened a storehouse
of classical Latin, meaning to liquidate the brute ignorance
held far and widely in such high
stock. The barbarism dominant in the Sciences
had to be supplanted by the power of grammar
which must be put good and green
in the window-front next to the truth and the word.

At the University of Salamanca, Elio Antonio de Nebrija
carried his argument, identified the field of battle,
challenged the phrase-mongers,
the masters who had Letters as their profession
and the habit of spitting out verbs from their mouths.
He provoked and defied, declared—in a war of blood
and fire—that the world is not just idle words;
if only we could speak the primordial tongue
we would recover Paradise.
Ignorance of it estranges us from the earth.

After quashing the grammarians, he crushed the jurists
who had not digested The Digests of Justinian,
attacked theologians who erred in their Scriptures,
put down the doctors of medicine confounded by Pliny
and the historians unacquainted with Spanish Antiquities.

From the masters—the languages of ox, dog, scrubbing
brush and viper—he studied the root of our tongue much
misunderstood in the voice man uses to articulate his ideas
till death swept over him in a babble of darkness,
for even the other world speaks a language of its own.

Second exodus from paradise

It isn't the slab of sacrificial stone,
it is down the side face
where they slit the sheep's throats.

It is the charnel house of cow-
calves opened into a channel
under the glazed roof of the morning.

It is the countryside of bone,
marrow and thighs,
the ribs and the hearts.

It is the skinned rabbits in the butchershop,
their legless racing
with meathooks through their heads.

It is the pigs on the spit
watching with the cooked whites of their eyes,
speaking with their snouts sewn shut.

It is the altar of the appetite
where the cow, the cock,
the sheep are sacrificed.

It is the woman in the man
called hunger,
the hunger for death.

1
Grey Whale

Grey whale,
once there is no more left of you than an image,
a dark shape moving on the waters
in animal paradise,
once there is no memory,
no legend to log your life and its passage
because there is no longer a sea where your death will fit,
I want to set these few words
on your watery grave:
Grey whale,
lend our destiny a new direction.

2
Dolphins

Brother and sister swimmers of the present,
by the thousands
the dolphins of the ancient myths
are killed by us in the sea.
Even in the ever-changing,
unremembering sea which we are and sail on
we must kill this sport
made in our likeness,
for if not
we will amount to nothing,
never able to fill the torn nets of our own greed.
In the sea, in the air, on the ground,
settling on a throne of ashes
we will govern
our black garden alone.

3

Tell me, hare up on the volcano,
tiger-striped butterfly among the ragged hills,
jungle bird of Lacandón,
dolphin deep in tropical waters,
the extinction of the species need not be
like the horrible hush in our desert.
Will our night be like that
across a paralyzed earth?

4

Animalia

What did the parrots in the wood
say before flying into the dark?
What did the sea turtles
say before finishing up on the sand?
What did the white-tailed deer
say before they beat it out of the brambles?
The golden eagle, the puma, the buzzard,
the otter, the quetzal, the spider monkey—what?
All we catch is their silence. Silence.

TRANSLATIONS BY GEORGE McWHIRTER

HOMERO ARIDJIS, BORN IN CONTEPEC, MICHUACÁN, IN 1940, IS PRESIDENT OF PEN INTERNATIONAL AND *GRUPO CIEN (ONE HUNDRED ARTISTS FOR THE ENVIRONMENT)*. A FORMER AMBASSADOR TO THE NETHERLANDS, SWITZERLAND AND EAST GERMANY, HE NOW LIVES IN MEXICO CITY WITH HIS WIFE, BETTY FERBER. HE HAS TWO DAUGHTERS, CHLOE AND EVA. WITH OCTAVIO PAZ, JOSÉ EMILIO PACHECO AND ALI CHUMACERO, HOMERO ARIDJIS EDITED THE SEMINAL ANTHOLOGY OF MEXICAN POETRY: **POESÍA EN MOVIMIENTO** (SIGLO VEINTIUNO EDITORES, 1966). HIS POETRY WAS FIRST INTRODUCED INTO ENGLISH THROUGH **BLUE SPACES** (SEABURY PRESS, N.Y. 1974), EDITED BY KENNETH REXROTH. ELIOT WEINBERGER'S TRANSLATIONS OF HIS WORK APPEARED AS **EXALTATION OF LIGHT** (BOA EDITIONS, NEW YORK, 1981). HE WON THE 1988 DIANA NOVEDADES LITERARY PRIZE FOR **MEMORIAS DEL NUEVO MUNDO**; **1492: THE LIFE AND TIMES OF JUAN CABEZÓN OF CASTILLE** (SUMMIT BOOKS, N.Y. 1990) WAS AWARDED THE GRINZANE CAVOUR PRIZE IN ITALY FOR BEST FOREIGN FICTION OF 1992.

THESE SELECTIONS ARE FROM **IMÁGENES PARA EL FIN DEL MILENIO, NUEVA EXPULSIÓN DEL PARAÍSO** (JOAQUÍN MORTÍZ, 1990), AND **POETA EN PELIGRO DE EXTINCIÓN** (EDITORIAL, EL TÚCAN DE VIRGINIA, 1992). SOME OF THESE TRANSLATIONS FIRST APPEARED IN *THE NEW REPUBLIC, MODERN POETRY IN TRANSLATION, LONDON MAGAZINE, HU (THE HONEST ULSTERMAN)*, AND IN *THE MALAHAT REVIEW*. TIEMPO DE ANGELES WAS PUBLISHED BY FUNDACIÓN CULTURAL, TELEVISA AC, 1994; IT'S FRENCH VERSION WON THE ROGER CAILLOIS PRIZE IN 1997.

ELVA MACÍAS (1944 -)

Presence

You come back into view—
a transparent body
trailing wings of bitterness

They beat at the door
eyes
stones
deep inside
the heart
they beat at the door
The hinges screech
blind sound of birds

Now your eyes don't bother you any more
they are two rocks
deep in a dry creekbed

The truce at Juchitán

After the battle
the smoke of death clings to us.
Its odour, like sulphur in a glass,
has choked the eyes of the enemy.

The immigrants

for Myriam Moscona

The gateway of ocean
closes.
Through it the immigrants passed.

The gateway to the land
opens.
New harvests after the battlefields.

The immigrants are hushed.
Their voice knows no echo in the square.
How lonely their faces are
in the magnificence of this light.

On Capricorn

You look after me,
you don't want me to lay cobblestones
into a steep hill,
to crown my braids with thorns,
feed on nettles.
You don't want me to breed pests,
you dread climbing up onto the roof.
But you can trace the ash mapped
in my skirts.
You know about spider webs
that can heal wounds
low in my belly.
You have seen the thin thread of blood
that flows from the index finger of my heart
when I write.

So you realize.
Our eyes slip off to sleep
in a different equinox.

70

Sign

What hand, opening, does not unfold its shadow?

For Aries

Here your calm enormity,
your habit of lounging like a leopard.
There your grand admiralty,
your cavalry.
Here the night watch on the fire,
your dialogue through the laughter
with those who are gone.
There your lichens
that caress my going adrift.
On high: the constellations;
and on your sleeping skin:
our homeland.

Game

You go around and around the almond tree.
At your steps
the partridge fly up
and out of the nighttime story,
a winged horseman and a hat
intimidate you.
It's your silent daylong game.

Far from memory

We are born, they say
on beds of cinders.
The tree sheds its high branches
of ash,
fragile as the weight
of their burning out in flight.

Open house

In the stables the animals are panting,
they have hauled in the benefits of the orchard:
the smell of freshly cut bales
invades the yard.
In the garden, peacocks, ducks
and plovers pick over the ground
between the roses, the almond trees, the tamarind…
Bare feet lavish their freshness on the corridors.
The customary fruit is laid out on the table
and everything is feasted with its task and spell of leisure.
Every morning
the doors swing wide,
both madmen and beggars sit back
in the hall
and travellers, without
lifting a latch,
secure a shelter from the midday sun.

The hacienda San Augustín

Cloister in ruins.
Gold falls in rays
of light over the big house
and into the dust between my hands.
Amid the ears of wheat a child is bewildered
by his own hay-coloured hair.
Commotion among those who seek him:
you are my son, Father,
my boy discovered in his temple.

The caravan of a young father

The carts are at rest under a frond.
You sleep at the verge of my madness, father,
you who work so hard.

At sunset
the men begin
to yoke their animals.

The afternoon comes in again,
giving way
to the caravan you captain.

Patriarch

Your roots point to the future,
testify to the nobility in our simplicity.

Along your boundaries the water is channelled
by the hands of men,

the animals herded together
by the voices of men,
and through those hard jobs
the loaves are multiplied.
Your kingdom exists
even beyond
the cussedness of insects,
the bonfire, the livestock,
the full harvest
that guarantees our stay here.

Pisces

Father, your feet—
ornate fish in their sandals—
slip cautiously
into the dark sea.
You yourself are the deep
that contains it all.
You search for a Sargasso Sea,
your place
to put down your life that is ending.
We are the long train that follows you
into a current you grew accustomed to
with the wisdom of the blind.
Since you no longer keep an eye on us,
we believe everything has changed.
But inside you, we are the same sea:
three children lashed to your clothing,
we shudder
while the rainy season
laid up in your shirt
flows through.

Today

I walk as far as the orchard
and forget that yesterday
someone wiped my body clean
of insects and grass.

The rooster on the balcony

A rooster sleeps on the balcony,
my daughter looks after it in the mornings.
And at night,
as soon as the poet in me sings
about how the flame floating between the two
is just a word,
once, twice, thrice the rooster crows
my betrayal.

Servant of the sea

> *... you came out of the carefreeness of the waters*
> *darkness was a halo dropped into your sleep ...*
> — Raúl Garduño

Before travelling to the other side,
your gaze crossed a copy
of the ocean and kept
a lookout over the rough weather of dreams.
A marine firefly
bursts in on the star you sail by,
the moon wraps your waist in jade,
and the small fish open the damp chorus
of their mouths.

Dolphin

The horizon of your skin
silver
dolphin.
A Mediterranean reverie, you are
a window to the animal that lays its lure for us:

the eyes of an icon
your word has the power
and your throne is made of mirrors.

Navigation

In the distance
       the fish becomes an eye
       that sails the sea through your brow.

Anchoring, the future lets out its roots
       and takes in the lines of its wisdom.

Faithful barque
       dozing you waited for the voices
       to weigh anchor again
       starfish dangling in amazement.

How long until the voyage is eclipsed?
       The sea is contradicted
       the first rock is born out of it
       and we run aground.

Nostalgia

A sunflower,
even plucked from its stem,
follows the sun's path faithfully.

Fishing

You are on one shore
of your likeness:
the sampan sail
of the wind flaps,
and parallel with the air,
runs a risk of harming you
if we haul in our nets.

Beside Li Tai Po Road

Under a tree
the wine and my heart
have gotten drunk on one another
and I sing.

Solicitude

Days of shy downpours.
I dare you to quit drizzling.
I dare you to wet me.
If you wipe out my footprints because you can't stand it
and the sun doesn't grimace all over my face
and I take good care of my raincoat
what do my feet trip along for
every day on the bus?
Where songs of suffering love
are worth sometimes twenty
sometimes ten cents
where my elbow rubs up against the point
of a black funeral umbrella, and my solicitude
gives up a seat for an old lady
who regards me with her religious magazine.
The articles make my hands sweat.
I get off before the corner
and walk along, worried.
What can I do with these moralities?

TRANSLATIONS BY **CAROLINE DAVIS GOODWIN**

ELVA MACÍAS WAS BORN IN TUXTLA GUTIÉRREZ, CHIAPAS, IN 1944. SHE STUDIED ARTS AND LETTERS IN CHIAPAS, MEXICO CITY, AND THE SOVIET UNION. SHE ALSO TAUGHT SPANISH IN THE PEOPLE'S REPUBLIC OF CHINA, WHERE SHE FLED IN 1963 AFTER FALLING IN LOVE WITH ERACLIO ZEPEDA, THE GREAT STORYTELLER AND MEMBER OF THE GROUP OF POETS KNOWN AS *LA ESPIGA AMOTINADA* (*THE REBEL EARS OF WHEAT*.) THE POEMS TRANSLATED HERE ARE FROM HER BOOKS **PASOS CONTADOS** (EDITORIAL VILLICAÑA, IZTAPALAPA, MEXICO CITY 1986) AND **LEJOS DE LA MEMORIA** (JOAN BALDÓ I CLÍMENT, EDITORES, 1989). "GAME," "BESIDE LI TAI PO ROAD," "FAR FROM MEMORY," "ON CAPRICORN" AND "SOLICITUDE" APPEARED PREVIOUSLY IN **PRISM** *INTERNATIONAL*, 33:3. A CHAPBOOK SELECTION OF HER WORK APPEARED FROM UNAM (UNIVERSIDAD NACIONAL AUTÓNOMA DE MÉXICO) IN 1992. HER LATEST BOOK, **CIUDAD CONTRA EL CIELO** (HUZAZUL, CONACULTA, 1994) WON THE CARLOS PELLICER PRIZE FOR POETRY. ELVA MACÍAS HAS LONG BEEN ASSOCIATED WITH UNAM'S CENTRE FOR LITERARY AND CULTURAL DEVELOPMENT (COORDINACIÓN DE DIFUSIÓN CULTURAL, DIRECCIÓN DE LITERATURA).

CAROLINE DAVIS GOODWIN IS A YOUNG WRITER LIVING AT A REMOTE SALMON HATCHERY IN SOUTHEAST ALASKA. SHE HAS PUBLISHED HER OWN POETRY IN *THE WHITE WATER REVIEW*, AND HER MOST RECENT POEMS FROM ALASKA APPEARED WITH HER LATEST TRANSLATIONS OF ELVA MACÍAS ("PISCES", "OPEN HOUSE", AND "SIGN") IN **PRISM** *INTERNATIONAL*, 36:1. IN 1998, **PRISM** AWARDED CAROLINE DAVIS GOODWIN THE EARLE BIRNEY PRIZE FOR THE BEST ORIGINAL POEMS PUBLISHED IN VOLUME 36.

ELSA CROSS (1946 -)

Bacchae

I

We submerged ourselves in the source.
We let our bodies into its current
like wandering banks,
earth detaching—carried off
the bulrush edges.
We flowed with its transparencies
and at the bottom of the riverbed
our legs brushed soft moss,
our feet tangled in weeds.
We felt the passage of those fish
which, when least expected, strike,
speaking between the thighs of the women.
And all the time in our ears the cadence
of a phrase strummed to its highest pitch.
Downstream we saw branches against the sky.
The sun sketched on our bodies
the shadows of the leaves.
The breeze carried your scent.
We passed under a willow
and its branches held by the hair
all the impulse downriver.

II

Surrounded by hills like walls

the men played on the terraces.
The sound of their races in the pastures.
A bruised blue in the air when the sun pushed through.
The birds were falling silent.
Bats lifted off into their erratic flight.
The men went galloping after goals in the game,
their cries echoing off the hills.
Applause.
They lifted you on their shoulders,
carried you downhill to celebrate.
At every exit from this village, a temple.
Seven doors, they said, guarded by archangels
and the one who hit the jackpot, got drunk in the portals,
spoke of heaven and hell,
as of places inside the body
but two inches apart.

III

Not your saintliest of souls.
The women awaited you like an advent,
and you arrived with marijuana in your pockets,
your hair mussed up,
barely escaped from who knows what raid.
And you had certain riddles,
as if in answer to the Queen of Sheba.
You laughed to see them so devout,
your bosom sisters,
and, like Shiva in the Forest of Pines,
unfurling an enormous phallus.
You seduced the high-minded
under the beards of their husbands.
And the women followed you.
Not one curse caught up with you,
O Smoker-of-Intoxicating-Weed.

Above, mirror-signals in the branches.
The earth quiet, waiting,
as on a feast day.
And over there the Concheros descended
with their pipes and their sad drums,
their rattles of dried seeds.
Dance of mirrors beneath the sun.
In the La Cruz quarter rockets thundered up.
Coloured banners hung from posts.
In staggering processions
the people went drunk through the streets
ready to topple on the uneven cobbles.
At night, the signal flares, your mirrors of smoke.
The rockets echoing like shots.
Adorers of fire.
On all sides we found
the rusted cartridges of bullets,
the scorch of gunpowder on the walls.
The children blew on their pinwheels,
blew on flowers,
set the petals flying with their breaths.
The women followed you.

IV

At cliff's edge we waited for the night.
The sight of the Conquistadors—had it not tracked
over the valley which lay at our feet?
Lights began to kindle,
our minds to dim,
then the vigil opened out its spider's belly,
its white goddesses.
We sated ourselves on wine and scents.
And every night a trial by fire,
like those Bards in the desert heights

by sheer force holding back threats divine
and atrocious.
Doubting if we'd get out alive from this tunnel,
from this night turned toward nothing.
We let pour down our throats
the sweetest wines.
Sated ourselves on honeys.
And in the height of the night,
the unheard-of grace in your body.
The world closed over our heads,
disappeared behind the rain.
We forgot to mind the children,
like the Bacchae
forgot our houses.
The rain on the mountain was a festival.
And who could predict we wouldn't be struck
by lightning?
Open transgression.
Such terror,
such beauty wrought around a void—
it sucked us in like the eye of a storm.
And you gave yourself to my delight.
Down we followed you to your caverns.
And at the bottom, only insects'
feet brushing our shoulders,
moths' wings.
And the fecund goddess
smothering us against her wet belly.
Lightning fell,
thunderbolts rolled across the sky
from the crest of the hills to the back of nowhere.
We were walking on air,
as if across a land-mined country.
And one explosion brought down on us such glory.

V

From town to town in ragged clothes
and windblown hair,
we ate, O Gods, your soma:
fungi full of earth.
We were under the volcano watching life's tumbling down.
Danger at every pass.
To drive such cold from the bones
we built bonfires of manure.
O mother cows.
Our beds of dung.
The earth trembled.
This day in the plaza bulls had killed men.
And from the heights
the sun was the pyre,
our bodies the offering,
those dying cicadas
the prayer.
And those drops about to fall to earth,
I take them in.
We saw the valley from the heights
and you were asking for fruit.
The clefts in the mountains, the fissures
made the wind sing.
That day the swallows came back
looking for the nests in the crag-tops.
We saw their signs.

VI

We migrated to the woods
like ascetics,
into an intemperate rigour.
Then another insanity seized those fleshless bodies,
the wide-open eyes,

the sunken cheeks.
The rope tightened to breaking.
Her mind flew away like a bird.
Went to the tree tops
to await sunrise.
But she stayed below,
joined her dry body to those thriving green worlds.
The cold salt of dawn in the sparrows' beaks.
She saw hummingbirds, the lacework of unidentified butterflies.
Death-Furies were feeding her.
She heard trumpets in the air
and screamed until she lost her voice.
About to die,
about to blind herself,
and sparrows crossed the sky as though nothing were up.
The world carried on the same.
Like ash swirling in the chimney, a rat
in its hiding holes, her mind alone
wandered. Soared up,
later. Lost sight of time,
sent her travelling the walls of besieged cities,
sent her shrieking from the stake,
sent her singing dressed in sackcloth
or to haunt miserable cafés under the Paris snows,
pianos stumbling through an ill-tuned waltz.
The bodies shrank back.
She screamed prophecies beneath the sun,
heard psalms,
cursed, and her spit withered the plants,
her thoughts could have struck you dead.
But still she could see those yellow birds,
migrants from the North.
They perched, singing, on a branch,
made love.

She ranted sleeplessly,
and inside her mind
another mind observed like an eye.
She flew off in search of her lover.

We turned into deer,
and crossed the woods like arrows.

VII

We were open wounds.
The feeling crazed us.
Your voice invented new registers in my ear.
Your musk intoxicated me more than wine.
The pleasure wounded us.
Inexhaustible,
drunk,
our bodies the offering
like fruit that women leave
on the southern beaches—that the sea takes.
We were lost to the world.
We drew boats in the air
and flew off in them.
All night long the boon of the sky
fell on us,
the rain over the trees,
and those drops gushing from the breast,
ah, our soma
—where did our bodies end?
—whose body was whose?
I felt my caress through your shoulder.
Your thoughts passed through my mind,
and where our desires met
firebirds appeared in the air.
I flowed inside you.
And who were you?

Only a mound full of bees,
water glinting like jewels.
Waves of sensation shook us,
we returned to the shore.
Such a vision of the sea to leave behind, such forests,
so much of your body.
A veil of flames spread behind the forms—
we were lost in staring into each other one moment more,
in the untimely flinching of your thigh.
Thus died the fish in the nets.

VIII

Your scratched face.
Under the market awnings,
a green glow on your brow.
Your eyes popping with so much fire,
such uncanny stopping places,
the platters of food we saw without seeing.
A green glow
as if it already reflected the trees,
already beheld the countryside out there
where you hoped to find one particular plant.
We searched in the volcanic rock
to find purple flowers growing from the stone,
delicate forms of cacti.
A whole countryside of pumice.
We made poor progress
and the afternoon blackened.
We spent the night under an apple tree.
Searched the mountain without trails.
And returned lacerated.
We searched without finding in the ruins
of pyramids, where you dropped off to sleep,
devourer of mushrooms, devourer of iguanas.

You snared me in your sleep,
made me slither.
My tongue slid out, sharp-tipped,
to gobble the ants crawling up your neck.
And your sweat smelled of mead.

IX

Scorpions came out at our passing:
white, shining on the worn floor.
We walked in silence
between broken balustrades,
our steps resounding in the vault.
Such dust along the roads which wound back here.
Something hurt us.
Words returning to the mouth.
Did we now have this taste for silence?
The long offering,
the involuntary propitiation
—did they then bear any fruit?
In the cloister,
spiderwebbed like mystical diagrams against the light,
the red-bloom of the flame trees.
We kept their seeds
and set passion flowers to dry in the window,
their coronas of purple pistils like thorns.
The wine brought on such a love for his Name.
Something opened a pregnable point in the chest,
a delight strange to our ways.
And drunk, at dawn,
chanting a lay in the garden,
you found your hair covered in dew.

X

Creepers with their blue flowers

in the blamelessness of this day
with not one cloud over August.
Dying of thirst,
rushing along a narrow road
with its guard-rails of red stakes at the sides,
we followed in a quintet,
the counterpoint of violas,
climbing the hill.
You uncorked bottles of wine.
And we were careful not to run the lambs over,
not to go falling headlong over the blink of an eye.
Guardian angels warned us
just in time, kept us from embedding
ourselves in the hillside.
Who were we pursuing like this?
Who following?
Detained at night by troops looking for guerrillas,
lit up by lanterns,
guns aimed at us.
Dozens of butterflies starred the windshield.
Ah, your offerings.
You put jasmine in the wine.
The inexhaustible wine,
even redder under the sun.
Or at night we drank sickening liquor
in bordellos on the outskirts.
Incessant celebration,
costing so much of our life,
our faces so pale.
And then, in every part,
the unquenchable smile
reborn,
O Rowdy, O Delirious One.
We drank musk from his mouth.

Our bodies burned, waiting one
moment too long, down to ashes.
And who could stop us?
Who could stop
those plants from climbing the wall?

XI

The vanity of time.
We pass the day
like vendors of necklaces,
birds of paradise,
ivory combs.
The branches of the trees bent under the rooks,
they painted the air black with their noise.
—And you, what do you think?
O Philosopher-bird.
The vanity of the day.
We pass our lives
like those animals we see
grazing the hills from sun to sun,
or listening to water fall through rocks.
Our posthumous sonatas.
Like those birds, we get lost,
hopping with drunkenness
through the branches day and night
into the delirium that peoples our roads
with phosphorescent creatures,
or throws up sparks at us like fireballs.

XII

Under ceilings of palm fronds we watched the sea:
the crabs creep ceremoniously among the rocks.
The wind shook our hair,
whipped the ceiling of palms.

The sea made itself heard,
smothered our voices
and chewed up the earth, leaving the wet
red roots of the palms bared to the air.
The taste of saltwater in the throat,
reddened eyes,
and growing drunkenness on the sand.
The heart listens only to itself.
Breath like a wave that comes and goes.
I feel the sand sticking to your skin,
your hair.
It comes and goes,
a wave which bursts,
a surf cresting in the throat.
The undertow seizes the heart,
rattles it
like small sea snails by the shore.
And something leads us to sink ourselves
deeper into the night,
that quagmire,
that echo in the depths,
coin which you toss into the well
and it takes a long time to strike the water,
echo in the deep.
And in this echo, once again, sea thunder.
Syllables without sense.
The heat on our bodies.

XIII

Oh-so-fickle ones, intoxicated,
with our gazes fixed
elsewhere, to propitiate
the Manes of another lineage,
we sate ourselves on beauty.

Drunk,
we listened with our flesh,
uttered strange modulations,
discordances.
A drop fell,
filtered through the rock,
honouring an unknown god.
From there we looked on the world,
a door guarded over by lions,
a conical tower open to infinity,
and the drop that falls
strikes our bodies,
the thrum of sistrums.
The sea, reeling, churned up by fire.
Blue venom in my throat.
The drop cutting deep into the image of my god,
filling the senses with its music.
A pause opened,
absorbed us instantly into silence.
The world halts at the centre of an axis.
Blades of fire surround.
Only the ascension,
nakedness.
The ten arms on your trunk carrying flames.
Your brow like the sun.
The beams spinning.
You dance
and all around nothing but ashes.
I too turn to ash,
I dance, I vanish.
And take hold of your body,
run through,
hollow as a reed,
I am the bed of a river,

a strength unfolding like a wing,
a thread of quicksilver,
a thin breath.
We spin on the heights.
The circulation of light.
There's not a breath of air.
We fly into the silence
in the opened void.
We are inside the lightning.

XIV

Not one image,
nothing to dictate a course,
save the trickle seeping through the rock,
overflowing into streams where we submerge ourselves.
And what we saw with our open eyes
broke away from the verges of the vigil
to flow into these transparencies.
Dissolution.
Offerings snatched by a wave.
We are as we descend—dissolving matter,
stellar dust.
Our breath inseparable.
Our sap untouched.
Oblation.
Dissolution.
An arm of a river bearing
heaps of dry leaves,
bewildered bees betweeen the flowers.
We are arms pierced by the wind,
hair undulating underwater,
bones laid bare.
Only skulls are we,
skulls of crystal, and inside:

galaxies, nebulae, pulsing stars.
A handful of ashes,
skeletons at the foot of the cliff,
the ghost of a willow,
a soundless voice.

XV

Through the atrium I walked.
The ground blanketed by violet campanulas.
The encounter lifting up my heart.
Inside the temple,
the seven archangels painted on the walls.
The May afternoon flowering.
The offerings to Mary
were drying out on the arc of triumph.
Sword in hand, Michael stood guard over the doors.
But we were not going into the temple.
"Tanto gentile e tanto onesta pare."
And when I looked round,
the grace of — Raphael? — in your smile.
I walked between the tombs
until I met you under the jacarandas.
The low brick walls were covered with purple flowers.
An ambiguous scent.
Below the walls the pig-keeper squealed.
The grunts of the swine carried into our talk.
And won't give a name to your frothings,
for poets lie too much.

TRANSLATIONS BY **KAREN COOPER**

ELSA CROSS WAS BORN IN MEXICO CITY IN 1946. SHE HAS A PH.D. FROM UNAM AND HAS STUDIED ORIENTAL PHILOSOPHY IN INDIA AND THE UNITED STATES. SHE HAS PUBLISHED TWELVE BOOKS OF POETRY: **BACANTES** APPEARED FROM ARTIFICE EDICIONES, MEXICO CITY, IN 1982. THREE BOOKS OF HER POETRY HAVE WON NATIONAL PRIZES. HER LATEST, **URRACAS** (EDITORIAL ALDUS, MEXICO CITY, 1995) WAS WRITTEN UNDER THE AUSPICES OF FONCA'S *SISTEMA NACIONAL DE CREADORES*. SHE HAS ALSO AUTHORED ESSAYS, MOST IMPORTANTLY, "LA REALIDAD TRANSFIGURADA EN TORNO A LAS IDEAS DEL JOVEN NIETZCHE," PUBLISHED BY UNAM, MEXICO UNIVERSITY PRESS. HER TRANSLATIONS INCLUDE **CANTO POR UN EQUINOCCIO DE SAINT JOHN PERSE**, UNAM-INBA.

KAREN COOPER LIVED IN ENCINAR DE LOS REYES OUTSIDE MADRID, SPAIN, FOR THREE YEARS AND IS CURRENTLY QUALIFYING FOR THE PH.D. PROGRAM IN COMPARATIVE LITERATURE AT THE UNIVERSITY OF BRITISH COLUMBIA. IN 1994, SHE WAS SHORTLISTED FOR THE CBC LITERARY COMPETITION IN NON-FICTION. HER POEMS HAVE APPEARED IN *JEOPARDY*, AND HER NON-FICTION, "WHAT SHE SEES," A BIOGRAPHICAL PIECE ON THE ARTIST, NORAH BEAUMONT, WAS PUBLISHED IN *FUGUE*. SHE HAS TAUGHT WRITING AND GIVEN WORKSHOPS AT REGENT COLLEGE AND AT FACE TO FACE, THE ST. JOHN'S ARTS FESTIVAL, AND IN VANCOUVER. SHE WORKED FOR A NUMBER OF YEARS AS THE EXECUTIVE DIRECTOR OF THE CHRISTIAN INTERNATIONAL SCHOLARS FOUNDATION AND AS A FREELANCE RESEARCHER AND EDITOR.

CARMEN BOULLOSA (1954 -)

Open

You made a marvel
of, with no harm to me, replenishing my clear water
with the liquor of the grape.
                              —Ramón López Velarde

I

Knife of light, cut
open fruit with which you turn
night into fire,
change flame into a fresh sense,
I come, seeking your breath,
the thirstier:
well of love—a pitcher
of day—that astonishes me.

II

Whole metal in the night without the shadow of a stone,
dark ink emptied into the ground,
mud—virgin, serene ...

Thing after thing beyond error,
every element intact,
before the yes, the no, before all form
like an emptied mould
or like a silver river with nowhere to pour,
beyond anyone's power to drink.

III

In you, the air is made nobler,
your skin—the fine sand on the shore,

your flesh—a wide sea,
and your love the sweetest, most harmonious tide.

IV

Deep water,
current that, without ever having seen the mountain,
          without knowing the jungle,
steers the sea blind
to landward.

Water that discovers me in its thousand ways,
always freer than sunlight.

V

Lake of two faces,
suspended sea,
all in the palm of your hand
like a grain of light,
incomprehensibly placid:

there's no urgency whatsoever, no time,
you are all possible space:
there is no distance.

VI

Nights of surly veils, your eyes:
my flesh, all a slow ejaculation,
is dying before them,
shut away from touch,
denied all doors
but like a mystery it finds you
inside itself,
a miraculous prayer,
nameless, forbidden alteration
that bids me surrender.

VII

In my ears, your body is a clear, fresh wind
that vamps upon itself.
The clean sound of breath and brass:

your lips ooze with lime,
your eyes are overlaid with mist
and this keen, tight-fitting thrall is your hand:
because the sea has nested in you, you are its guide,
and from you the dullest root drinks in its thorn:

for you are the wind,
and also, virgin rock
hidden many metres deep.

VIII

Light of lights, your outspread trunk has dubbed you
and your perfume, your scent of simple grass and lilac,
your fresh mouth
calls you mischievously by your name.

IX

Clear petal on the flower you lean over,
coastline into the dense jungle you gaze down at,
edge of steel against steel you bear down on,

faithful root you imitate the stem, the flower,
            the aromas,
            spill back in around you.

That, but the smooth petal too, taste of colour
            and perfumes,
the coast as open as any mouth,
the steel, tensile and honed,
the root, solid, full of power and the glow
of giving:

so are you, love;
so you and I, two lovers' and loving surrenders.

X

A calabash is your fresh mouth
wineskin of syrup
a strain of fresh love that smitten with you
turns the death and deceit
back into flesh, into love.

XI

You are no feather
bending before the wind,
no lukewarm neck of a goose,
no shy skin of a peach;

you are a graft of all this tenderness
on the mightiness of a mountain,
the pounce of a pent-up feline.

XII

The earth's embrace,
the certainty of what mountain put a name to,
secret made voice,

the silence is your cuneiform breath,
your fragrances and your body are
the calligraphy of the gods, thirsting after love.

XIII

Peach,
honey of grape,
fibre of persimmon:

you offer me a glossary of flesh
in every kiss.

XIV

The pitchfork of the wind:
metallic as a bolt of light
you have homed into the cedar
at the same time as you lay, docile, on the flower,
a kiss of fecund passion.

XV

Feral fruit of the field and the day,
your desire is the untameable S-
blade that, on this spot, cut to size
what I wear for a body.

XVI

Your breath, distinct
scent of burnt grass,
the licit perfumery of species which,
the goblets of immense trees, you have stirred through
into the whole night.

XVII

Your body is always right,
lucid frond,
sap which brings me back to life.

XVIII

Foliage,
tomenta of the world,
that gives body to the desert
and soul to the uninhabitable sea.

XIX

Wave of fresh nights,
alfalfa galore:

your look, your dark eyes spill all
of your love onto this bed.

XX

You have tumbled the wall down,
left me
like a doe at bay
on the day of the hunt.

XXI

Coupling of fire,
speak;

tell me how many wagons you need
for hauling your kisses
from one body to another.

XXII

Take this noontime, double and lunar,
for in your breast the world is multiplied.

XXIII

Candy,
sunflower oil:
in your hands I appear
all dressed up as food and salt.

XXIV

Sieve that filters my feelings,
that only lets desires and kisses through,
grain that germinates in the heart:

insane wonder,
it only takes an eyebrow for my breath to quicken.

XXV

Mandrake root,
in the total darkness
of this awkward heart, you know
how to attune
to the dead body (all dead bodies)
without dread,
to set my soul free of the dead.

XXVI

Top floors, scissors,
cyanide, the hangman's rope
you'll do away with,

for you can charm fiend
or foe into the sincerest friend.

XXVII

Lark,
you soar so high

but how do you hold on—
tight as a ring,
as comfortable as a pair of stockings—
to my hands, to my legs?

Poems out of childhood

I

1

The pyracantha gave me a bite to eat.

Poison!
A flower's bit me.

Corolla and seeds crumble over my lips.

I ploughed into the lewd calix of a plumbago until I left it
nectarless.

A flower's bit me.
The wing tumbles off a bumblebee onto my head and melds
into the scalp.

—"Did you ever see a dragonfly landed on your lawn?"—

Much worse than poison.
Who could bear having the Devil buzz
about his awful sewing?

Poison. Something worser than poison
in a pyracantha, a plumbago
in those Devil's darning needles.

2

A floor, spotless and smooth.

—Shake out your dress before putting it on
in case spiders, scorpions . . .
—"Cockroaches can't breathe, can they?"—
I hear them gasp before they take off, sprightly.
—"No, don't hit . . . no, don't hit—
her! —The scorpion that's tramping up her dress."—

103

Shake it out before it's put on.
Tip the shoes out before they're slipped on.

Floor smooth, but sneaky.
Same goes for walls.

3

The juice of the orange peel burned on the wrist.

They tell tales about how bees
squeeze into their house, get stuck
together and gobble up the ladies'
legs and foreheads.

They tell how the stream out of their house ends up
in with the rose bushes and the crickets.

The orange peel juice (the burn mark on the wrist),
a regular scalding
and whole big story, gone unheeded,
as savage as a dog running in under the trees.

4

Cricket hunt

Merce, Isabel,
all you've got to do
is gawk at a bit of bush
till it's awake, Merce,
Isabel, till you're fed up.

How expectantly the leaf wakes
              arthropod
in the shape of a cricket.

Leaf soup and we let 'em have it wide awake.

A hole in the lawn

with water and a spoonful of sugar
and the crickets
                    —Squash 'em, Mercedes
                    Drown 'em, Isabel—
We got to let those wakened-up leaves have it
down our hole in the lawn.

II

1

Lifting from the palm of my hand
          (it's my skin
          my fingerprint)
the bird flies off
          — where?

I get up, I slip out the bars to the door.

I clutch at a hot handful of feathers like a scream.

It's gone.

          —where ?
          Where's my parakeet gone and died?

2

(On the garden wall)

Gustavo and I are perched on the garden wall.
It isn't a wall, it isn't a bank,
it's an immense look.

I see. I laugh: I've never been so far away from home before.

3

Slips, falls (slowly), lets out a scream…
gets up. Who heard?

Who got hit, where? We heard, didn't we?

Then Papá decided to buy plastic mats
                              for the shower.
And the scream?
Who can fix a scream?

4

The bat of an eye
No. No, I don't see.
It's like you'd pitched me facefirst into a puddle of mud.

5

Beneath your nightie something dark lurks between your legs

      . . . none of us, none,
      but none of us will say "we"
      we won't let   anyone . . .

It makes you swell, coarsens your skin,
distends the trunk about the breasts,
the hips, the waist,
takes all resistance out of the skin,

      . . . none of us is going to swell,
      have the skin break out,
      we won't let it.

6

Step on a crack get a whack
      (cheer up,
      immense flagstones of the schoolyard
      anyone who steps there steps very rarely)
—step on a crack
get yourself a whack.

7

The boozer

His drool itches across my face
                        till it reaches the lips.

8

Naked

After lifting my skirt at the sound
I deserve to have death lift the skin off me.

TRANSLATIONS BY ARTHUR LIPMAN

CARMEN BOULLOSA WAS BORN IN MEXICO CITY IN 1954. SHE STUDIED HISPANIC LANGUAGE AND LITERATURE AT THE IBEROAMERICAN UNIVERSITY AND AT UNAM, AND WAS AN EDITOR FOR EL COLEGIO DE MÉXICO ON THE **DICCIONARIO DEL ESPAÑOL EN MÉXICO**. IN 1983, SHE FORMED TRES SIRENAS WORKSHOP PRESS. IN 1989, SHE WON A XAVIER VILLAURRUTIA AWARD, AND IN 1991 A GUGGENHEIM FELLOWSHIP. AT SAN DIEGO STATE UNIVERSITY, SHE WAS A DISTINGUISHED VISITOR FOR 1990 AND WRITER-IN-RESIDENCE AT THE KUNSTLERPROGRAMM OF THE DAAD, BERLIN, GERMANY, IN 1995. SHE WAS THE 1997 RECIPIENT OF THE LITERATURPREIS OF FRANKFURT AND ANNA SEGHERS PRIZE. SHE HAS BELONGED TO THE SISTEMA NACIONAL DE CREADORES DE MÉXICO SINCE 1992. NINE BOOKS OF HER POETRY HAVE BEEN PUBLISHED. THESE SELECTIONS ARE FROM **LA SALVAJA** (FONDO DE CULTURA ECONÓMICA, 1989). HER MOST RECENT VOLUME IS **LA DELIRIOS** (FONDO DE CULTURAL ECONÓNIMCA, 1998). MANY OF HER PLAYS HAVE BEEN PRODUCED OR PUBLISHED AND TWO NOVELS ARE AVAILABLE IN ENGLISH: **THEY'RE COWS, WE'RE PIGS** (GROVE PRESS, NEW YORK, 1997) AND **THE MIRACLE WORKER** (JONATHAN CAPE, LONDON, 1995). SHE LIVES WITH HER HUSBAND, ALEJANDRO AURA, AND THEIR CHILDREN IN MEXICO CITY.

ARTHUR LIPMAN IS A RETIRED FINANCIAL CONSULTANT LIVING IN VANCOUVER. BORN AND EDUCATED IN ENGLAND, HE LIVED IN BRAZIL FOR TWELVE YEARS. A COLLECTION OF HIS SONNETS, **SAUDADES**, WAS PUBLISHED IN BRAZIL IN 1939. HE IS A THREE-TIME WINNER OF THE ANNUAL SALMON ARM SONNET COMPETITION AND HAS RECEIVED SEVERAL AWARDS FOR HIS LIMERICKS IN THE STEPHEN LEACOCK AND HALIFAX LIMERICK CONTESTS, WHERE HE RECEIVED 1ST AND 2ND PRIZES IN 1996. HE TRANSLATED **O LADO FATAL**, A COLLECTION OF LOVE POEMS BY THE BRAZILIAN POET LYA LUFT, SOME OF WHICH HAVE BEEN PUBLISHED IN **EXCHANGES**.

VICTOR MANUEL MENDIOLA
(1954 -)

The fish tank

to Orlando

1

The fish, in the large dome
of the sea,
breathes at the clouded
bottom of the air.
Below a colour
of salt and suns
he scarcely moves.
He is a dense particle
of light;
the pearl in its glass case.
My eye delights in the fish
on his altar of foam.

2

In the oxygen of the room
I watch how you move
between the blue planes
of your skin,
the fins of a transparency,
on wings of the water,
I fly in this fish bowl.
I fly in the eyes of the thought.
here you breathe,
here I watch over you,

Here I give you life
under the round glass
of my room.
You are the blue fish
in the clenched fist of my hand.

3

to Manuel and Horacio

The fish rests.
In the tank,
light sketches
a watery sky.
There is not one
particle asplash
nor the pitch of one wave,
nor a single gram
of squall or cloud.
All is silence
in this oxygen.

4

After many hours of sleep,
you open your eyes.
Look at the room
that (in some way) also
is sleeping,
eyes closed,
body napping,
light sheltered
in its cave.
The dwelling
and you breathe
together.
The light, in her,

breathes too:
air on the inexplicable
glass of this tank.

You open your eyes,
leap for the light,
blow away the ring
of this bubble.
The dwelling and you
breathe dreams
together.

5

to Coco Alcocer

In the bowl of this light
—the room lit
with one small lamp
—I repeat my pointless underwater swimming.
Smash nostrils against the glass,
place eye to the mouth
of the oceanic bottle,
push head above the water line;
a dorsal fin
draws circles,
a back questioning its engulfment
without reply in the depths
of the glass dome;
like the shark
I bruise the face.
Fish and perplexity
give flight to my thoughts.

Oration

The music on the radio. The car. The rain.
It rains. I watch the solitude of the water
through the windshield; unhurried thirst.
Everything falls, settling in easily

on the brightness of this supine vision
under the rain; a syllable in a short,
soft voice moves my thoughts.
The water runs on outside with its mass.

I pray. I repeat the phrase
where, between my lips,
God is water, the word
deciphers my voice and drinks me in.

I don't know what things I say with my voice,
I speak to the solitude, I tell it to open.
The music on the radio. The car. The rain.

Entranced

A murmur of insects among the leaves.
Thoughtfully, you listen—leaning
on the black sill of the window—
to the fugue that rises up from the ferns.
You listen to the crickets, feel sorry
for the spider in its web, you follow the wind
into the night . . . night is stirring in the shadow
and you listen to its abundance.
From the street comes the backfire
of cars, feverish words, the disdain in the noise

of things. But you remain entranced
in the fierce din of the ferns,
remote and still in the uproar
of leaves.

August

In plants, there is something that rests,
perhaps preserving some strength
or some health that it disperses
toward the air . . . and the hot afternoon.

The hour strikes. The lemon is weightless
in the light of the garden: says its piece
with green slowness, and in each thing
uncovers me in the languor of my idleness.

The creeping vine

Lying on the grass of the garden
the creeping vine caught my attention.
I held my head in my hands
in order to study its impulse to root.
In its flight the rhythm of the shadows
concentrates and the insects flow
through the leaves. I understood
through her the healthiness of the surprise.
Before the marvel of the green vegetal curtain,
I was taken aback. Its exuberance shook me
continuously. And I understood its primitive
silence, its obstinate slowness, its gloom,
its grave notes and its enormous flight.

The light listens

You are asleep. You wake to dreams.
Walk as far as the window. Open it.
Leaning-out-of-it pleases you
to observe that wilderness of grass
you listen to in the garden—the air rests
between the branches and the creeping vine.
Before your eyes the foliage trembles
in the yellow plum trees.
It appears that you speak, but you continue—
separate in the dream within your dreams
—where you are awake.
I watch you sleep, trace the paths
of your breath. The leaves tremble,
the light listens. I wake asleep.

Sea

You are there, on the other chair.
You live a world apart
on the opposite side of the table.
Your glances are there,
your cries are
birds that return
from the sea out there,
your hands wander
over the table
like tireless nomads
in the blue expanse.
I write in Morse,
send up smoke signals,

I set off a bottle from the shore
of this sea, I send my armies
to conquer
the sacred lands out there,
I seize the burning coals
out of the same dream.
But you go on out
to the end of so much accumulated sea.

The puppets

You pull a string
and I lower my head
to kiss you;
you raise another
and my arms encircle you,
I say that I love you;
you tighten another
and our bodies
open their lips,
love opens its stores,
we burn in the faint
dunes of ourselves,
the sun fills us,
in the eclipse of a cloud,
we are lost; again you pull a string
and the fire turns against us,
illness and death,
the room lonely, without light,
without words,
blame, bad omens;
you pull a string again

and a tree stops us,
the peace silenced,
the peace on high.
From my position,
I am drawn out,
the cords that I tug
with closed fists;
I topple the puppets over
and you fall along with me
like a thirsty bird
and I feed you,
cover your eyes,
caress your thighs,
surround you with sounds
of love and fear
and you take wing into
I don't know what happiness.
Once more you pull the strings,
steaming,
I scarcely cover you
in shadow;
you repeat you love me.

Too much sun

This morning there is too much sun
for the dead.
They clench
their fists and their eyes
but the sun increases;
they roll over
on the ground, eat dust,
and the sun gloats over them in the light;
they are silent once more
but the sun continues
its dazzling eloquence;
they forget
and beg its forgetfulness,
but the sun sticks to
its calendar;
they never speak
but the sun speaks forever;
they die more
but the sun brings
the most luxurious springs.
How to stop so much light
—they exclaim between one brilliance and another,
among the huge illuminations.
How to stay without saint or sign
—they repeat to one another
in their hermetic beds.
But the sun strengthens
and they can only clench
their eyes and fists
and die each day
a little more.

Like the sea

The dead beg
an answer.
The living watch and say nothing.
The dead are anxious,
speak of their world of shadows,
speak of all that is silent
and troublesome.
Explain, argue
the theology of the missing sun,
of the charred sun.
They go to the blackboard,
write the word dead
in many ways
and whisper in the ear
of the living.
The ear grows and grows
until it envelops the dead.
Then the living
listen to a murmuring of the sea.

Doubles

Dream of death and dream of crocodile.
Like old friends they speak in pauses:
one listens and the other is a reflection,
both enjoy the healthiness of the Nile.

1 have let my eyes and my tongue go
and in the sunshine of my dreams watch over them.
The whole moment stays suspended,
doubled in the double of a mirror.

Now two is eight in noble faces:
two crocodiles, two dead, two rivers
and the tongue, the divided tongue.

The visions doubled by the cross-eyed god
dreaming beneath a sun of two summers
and learning death aforehand.

Poetics

Language moves in through the eye: adjusts
image for tooth and palate, delicately.
Samples the landscape and sucks in
patient water from the river. The exact look

is opened in the voice or out of the light raised up
toward the same language. Everything registered
on the retina is a gloss of the soul
to cure and renew us.

Alighted on one thing, language and eye are the bird
that lifts off in the light on my balcony,
a descending from the air that touches us.

It is the song of the unknown
soon become a vision.
The eye moves, bilingual, in through the mouth.

The tree

From my room
you can see a tree.
I rest quietly
on the bed,
the tree likes to sprawl out on the air;
I open my eyes
—its green enters—
the tree turns elastic
and inside of me
the leaves grow damp;
I see the bustling of the wind
among its fronds
as it perceives
that slender murmuring of the soul;
I live like
the birds descending
to the strongest and most uplifted arms
and, winged like those same birds
discover the ascent
of happiness.

The hard-boiled egg

to Tomas

From the small basket I take the fragile egg.
Weigh its roundness in my hand,
white, weightless—as hushed and deep,
as gold and ogre as the middle ages.

I carry it to the pot with a spoon

and hide it in the boiling; measure time
and watch how fear sinks into the deep:
to be old and hard in a frail renewal.

All is the white shape of astonishment.
The never-to-be-pecked trapped,
and the cock sent down to the dungeon,

the egg is the note of another song
the shell holds an ogreless gold:
my supper, an old hard-boiled egg.

TRANSLATIONS BY SYLVIA DORLING

VICTOR MANUEL MENDIOLA WAS BORN IN MEXICO CITY IN 1954. HE STUDIED ECONOMICS AT UNAM. HE IS CO-DIRECTOR OF THE PUBLISHING HOUSE EDICIONES EL TUCÁN DE VIRGINIA. HE HAS WON PRESTIGIOUS INBA-FONAPAS (1980-81, 1997-98) AND MEXICAN CENTRE FOR WRITERS GRANTS. THESE TRANSLATIONS ARE FROM **EL OJO** (EDITORIAL VUELTA, EDICIONES HELIÓPOLIS, MEXICO CITY, 1994). PREVIOUS BOOKS INCLUDE **POEMAS** (EL TUCÁN DE VIRGINIA, 1980), **SONETAS A LAS COSAS** (OASIS, 1982), **TRIGAL** (WITH OTHERS—UNAM, 1983) AND **NUBES** (FONDO DE CULTURA ECONOMICA, 1987). WITH MANUEL ULACIA AND JOSÉ MARÍA ESPINASA HE EDITED AN ANTHOLOGY OF CONTEMPORARY MEXICAN POETS, **LA SIRENA EN EL ESPEJO** (EL TUCÁN DE VIRGINIA, 1990).

SYLVIA DORLING'S WORK HAS APPEARED IN *WHETSTONE, VINTAGE 95* AND MOST PROMINENTLY IN *NEW QUARTERLY*, WHICH FEATURED AN ESSAY BY DORLING ON HER POETRY IN THE 1996 WINTER ISSUE; THE SUMMER '97 ISSUE OF *NEW QUARTERLY* INCLUDED ONE OF HER SHORT STORIES. SHE WAS THE FIRST PRIZE WINNER OF THE 1995 NORMA EPSTEIN AWARD FOR A VOLUME OF VERSE ENTITLED **AVIARY**. SHE WAS BORN IN KINGSTON, ONTARIO, AND NOW LIVES WITH HER HUSBAND, RICHARD, IN NORTH VANCOUVER. SHE HAS A MARRIED SON, MATTHEW; HER YOUNGEST SON, WILLIAM, STILL LIVES AT HOME.

Francisco Hinojosa (1954 -)

Robinson at bay

1

A quick cuff of air
so the sun will
think twice about its ease.

No more exhaling or looking dead-ahead:
no more dazzling.
To not see. Perhaps, to have the eyes blasted out.
To not speak or think new words.
Let it dazzle on,
even though it may mean, eventually, to go blind?

Light draws its outline
over the closed eyelids—
a far arch, aflame,
that pours down behind the mountains.

Light breaks the circle
and draws its gaze along the coast,
emerging from the socket of the eye.

2

I made way on a boat at bay,
and for months on end looked only out to sea.
Night after night I drank in the insomnia of the crew
—still smarting from their farewells,

fond adorers of our what-was,
elbows still leaning on the smooth rail of what-is-to-come,
and I looked at myself: alone,

protected in a cloak of round and invisible ocean.
I could hear the slow advance, the brake, the nagging immobility,
a song threshed from the wet saltpeter,
the crystal in its sparkle.

Through the thuds of water I thought about the darkness,
about rocks diluted by the night,
about my weakness and my want,
about finding myself adrift without instruments.

Though we carried bay windows aboard,
bundles, ropes, needless pieces of furniture,
near-new appliances,
an old photograph album
—images and more images; just stones:
wastelands met all over again in town squares,
valleys, trees poking through,
sunsets stamped onto the mosaics,
eyes like statues of water,
father, mother, children
in the blissful night of the abortion—
I carried a cup, long and slender,
with shadows of friends,
cheeses, fresh waters, marmalades,
scents—wind-chilled, bittersweet.

I remembered.
I bit, one after another, into familiar bodies on the threshold of
            death,
into the innards of the old poets,
in the graveyard where I played at dyeing my skin with bone dust.
That much, yes, is true,
all alone among the splendours,
thus did Robinson, the hunted,
sleep under cover.

3

The boat was then a priceless object
in the museums of the Pacific.
The night a dragon weathervane pointed West.
The Ocean: a tomb,
skeleton of a landless wind,
evidences of our exile were
the bones of boys,
of prostitutes,
of loves with no cheeks on them,
of exiled mates who never got a ship to weigh anchor,
of boneless old men,
of judges who legislate the displacement of Barbarians,
of savages gone astray on the desert sands,
of Barbarians,
of a friend dead,
of an amorous cook, agonizing over the dead friend,
of a mother and father dead,
of all the civilized and their thoroughfares,
of the gods on riggings sunk, undersea, as deep as the fish
and who return now unsmilingly to Virgil's ancient face.
The destination was a labyrinth of fish.

4

Winter and nineteen-seventy-seven,
at the bow of the boat,
and along with Polyphemus, his back to me, brooding.
The Cyclops arrived from the outcrops of Aetna
to share his idleness and wine
when it struck the hour in which the storm clears
and his blindness might just have been a quick swipe of air—
a not-looking, before the words.

All day, the Cyclops stumbles after the ship:
he is cold.

Behind the meandering tracks of our steps, his eye melts
and he wishes to talk about unpredictable skies,
about the ice age of the species.
More man than giant,
he gathers the crew together
to tell tales of the gods' painstakingness,
the labours and the centuries,
the toughness of human flesh in its voracious adolescence.

He carries a glass box, like his own special insomnia,
it is slivers of a poisonous damp;
his veins are the many other segments to his strength
and his skin—tempered eucalyptus:
he wants to be overwhelming,
puncture his neck
and offer a narrow entrance, there, for the Horse.

"Haul on the ropes," roars the monster,
"Pull up the anchor."
But no.
We will do no new kidnappings, make no more war.
There are no Helens now.
Time has run out, Polyphemus.

At the bow of the boat and in the Cyclops' cellar,
my breathing is coupled to the damp wood:
it's the right moment to open the eyes,
widen the pupils like nets spread out over the night
and let the pupils
—allow these terraqueous orbs,
the eyes to be shocked by the gloom that dwells in parallel
            rooms.
A soft sputtering of wax:
for the last time the sun drips down the hollow in the armour.

Let them pop out of their sockets now.
Beloved Polyphemus, divine giant.

At the moment of eventide's greatest bounty
when the wood, drying, traces its wounds with the noise:
sheds its bark in a motion, like bleeding away,
the walls tumble in,
slivers fall across the belly,
the arteries collapse in heavy convulsions:
motion consumes itself,
spills out into one last breath veering westward.

I notice the bitter scent of sage,
imagine the slow advance, the brake, the nagging immobility.

5

Winter is now a spectre, its stature reaching
way down to the sea bottom.
We're at the level of blind fish
by the time the boat finishes the required meanders,
it has rounded the island,
it sets the land afire so as not to self-destruct
and will not look to for'ard:
near the cliffs, one of the crew
       wastes his whole mortal time hidden
       in the rocks.
Twenty-eight years of bated breath,
a few seconds for the drop,
nine days to see Crusoe's body make its landfall of the shore,
hard by a fish that had entered its vegetal cycle already;
he was floating without his thick goatskins,
from their three millennia of occidental moons stripped naked
       now.
We had to do penance for the last leg,
scrub down the sepulchre.

6

(Fragment from Robinson's log-book)

"Sun, release me from gravity. Cleanse my blood of the heavy moods that protect me . . . it's true, from my excesses and foolishness, but which thwart the whole thrust of my youth also and dampen my joy in living. When I confront my face in the mirror, sad and misty with its far-northness, I understand the two senses of the word grace, that—which applies to the dancer and which concerns the saint—can be united under one particular Pacific sky. Teach me your light-heartedness, and the smiling acceptance, without aforethought of the boons immediate in this day, without gratitude, without fear.

. . . I am an arrow shot straight into your hearth, a plumb line whose perpendicular bob has defined your dominion over the globe, gnome of the solar quadrant, over which a needle of shadow inscribes your progress.

I am stood up, your witness on this earth, your flame-tempered sword."

Michel Tournier
Friday or Doldrums in the Pacific

7

April and nineteen-seventy-eight,
the evening vanishes an hour after the storm.
Voices rise up out of everywhere,
their lost complicity is knit back again:
they are simply happy,
laughing inexhaustibly as they bail water from the boat.
The crew rests their weariness,
it is like steam dancing on their lack of sleep.

From the terrace I watch the play of shoulders,
light, sharp weapons clashing,

the sea boils alongside the wine of glory:
sea-wine,
time-wine to be drunk ashore,
grape-wine,
the soluble wine of nakedness.

Every last one of the women have come
to toast the doings in the abyss,
have come deprived of their heavenly bodies,
with every dish and pitcher,
with the skeletons of their eyes on platters,
with polar opposite lips and orange-tinted stares,
with peals of foreign moistness,
with the tropics in their hips,
with laughter in their sex,
they come singing with the bellows of other seas,
lunatic, loving, feminine,
they come slipping in,
come with their troubles and jasmine.

From the terrace I observe:
a fine rain overflows the cage;
they all fall into the water
and bite the fish flying by;
the mist is settling
on a hospitable sea,
and the crew thinning out.

8

May and mild midday:
the boat, thus far, wanders at its whim.

Someone comes out singing:
a woman in a grey tunic lagging behind;
she goes skipping by and barefoot,

takes a little saliva and washes off the sea,
then gathers up its foam to weather her face.
The ritual is carried out with kindly quietness,
thirst satisfied in slow sips
and the look dissolved into the beach she has won over:

      a long, steep path up,
      the clatter of broken and weather-worn bricks,
      a church under construction,
      the old sea hurling three salt syllables against the coast,
      a horizontal sun.

And her again.
She irons a dress made of air now:
an orange-buttoned breeze
for her wedding day.

9

Then, to the books:

      "The earth is a sphere that has a gravity without apples."
No. Surely it's flat from here to the horizon. Splash splash splash
the muffled sigh of water doing tumbles.

(Splash: the water folds over the rocky walls, it thins and voices
gush up: conches and shingle; it rubs and wears away, chisels,
scratches its belly, chatters and gnaws; a moment passes and
another slap of water caresses the shoreline with liquid hands.

Splash—back on course, more regular than ever; water falls in a
melée, it is a falling in bursts, it throbs with fury before the pounce,
returns and once more thins; the aquamarine dissolves,
the crabs taste of salty mint.

Splash—where are the inlets, the arms of the river, the water's eyes?)

10

Their form is already a bit of evidence.
Bodies, boat, stones on the road.
Their loves remain, chamomile, the rituals of language,
a warm, sandy verb remains,
abandoned by the tide.
Hung out next to the oldest of suns,
the sound dries and stays hidden,
without sheen,
behind the word hill.

A shout,
a sharp noise,
an agreement,
the din afterwards.

Then, once more, the sea kicking up the beach.

TRANSLATIONS BY **RAÚL PESCHIERA**

Franciso Hinojosa was born in Mexico City in 1954. He has edited *La gaceta* (Fondo de Cultura Económica) and *Universitarios* (Universidad Nacional Autónoma de México). He is a member of the Sistema Nacional de Creadores. "Robinson at bay" was first published in a collection with the same title and has been anthologized in Spanish by Evodio Escalante in **Poetas de una generación 1950-1959** (Premia, Coordinación de Difusión Culutral, Dirección de Literaturea/ UNAM, Mexico City, 1988) and in **La Sirena en el Espejo/The Siren in the Mirror** (el Tucán de Virginia), edited by Espinasa, Mendiola and Ulacia. He has published three books of short stories—**Informe negro, Memorias segadas de un hombre, en el fondo bueno y otros cuentos hueros y Cuentos héticos**—and a large number of books for children, among them: **A golpe de cal- cetin, Joaquín y Maclovia se quieren casar, Cuando los ratones se daban la gran vida, y Amadís de anís, y Amnadíz de cordoniz.**

Raúl Peschiera is a young Vancouver writer of Peruvian origin who edits *The Review: A Journal of International Literature*, which is distributed in hard copy and on disc programmed for Adobe Reader. He also holds an MFA in Creative Writing from McNeese University, has had his poetry published in translation in the Parisian magazine, *passage d'encres*, has published criti- cal work on Czech poetry in *Slovo*, a University of London publication, and has recently com- pleted "The Shining Path," a book-length poem about Abimael Guzmán, the Peruvian revolution- ary. His translation of "Robinson at Bay" first appeared in *Modern Poetry In Translation*, London, England.

MYRIAM MOSCONA (1955 -)

Tangier

Where's the lady?
Where are the females?
Where are the market women headed for?
How many scorpions are there under their shawls?
Who parted the fabric of their veils?
Can they manage to see me through the fine mesh enfolding
    them?
Do they hate the surprise that stares at them?
Do they fling off their wraps at night?

They talk among themselves.
The guttural sound muffled under the cloth
but they do go mad with talk in the streets.
Sometimes they come to a stop
in front of a fig stall.
Laugh to themselves.
The hubbub: a collective zeal
pushes them along.

On Fridays
they perform the dance of the damned.
Ah, the eyes. What do they do to fill them with fragrance?
Do they live a parallel life in dreams?
Do they inscribe a memory of haste on their sepia bodies?
Or just make do.
They spread their legs and are the spans of bridges.
They wake. They sleep. Go back to the Kasbah
to gaze at the red figs, scare away a cloud of flies.
When no one is watching they slip their hands beneath their
    shawls.
Silently compare their bodies.

They are slyly confectioning their boredom
buying and selling the cardamon
between belches of a bittersweet essence.
They walk quickly.

The yammer
(do you hear it though the words?).
The summer turning them into shadows.
Far, far away, their lamentations fade.

Fez

for Adela Revelo

If there were a stranger
able to steal away into his own oily tongues
would he deposit anything under the cloth?
Which lubricant, which ointment?
Which almost imperceptible balm would he choose to sate them?

His unfound amours hide under the veil.
They have not yet been held down on the flat metal tables of partum:
have hardly dreamed of the adulterer who will slip them the poison.

A woman

She hides her heart
so she can walk in the desert
She draws her sex in the sand
and waits for darkness

Tetuan

Wood-colour eyes
hard as walnuts
hold a kernel of calm in their depths.
They recall the whip
they were trained with.

As a compass the earth
their feet the toes
feel their way
like insects.

Tall torsos
       short torsos
halted one next to the other
they are whole establishments
cities of intrigue
sixteenth century tapestries.
They tuck children into their message bags.
Loyally some dog is guarding them.

Who hid the mirror that keeps them from being seen in detail?

The house, dwelt in by other errand girls,
releases the tumblers in its locks at noon.
Between one laugh and the next, they fly out.
Will they be the traffic of an unended childhood?

They find their bearings with their fingers
count with their fingers
bring up kids
love centipedes
embroider dresses with cotton thread.
Generous

rooted in silence
they howl themselves hoarse in bed.

Inside their eyes of wood,
a stave of ocular music,
they choke.
Do they let it burst out in the night
when they soak their feet in pools of lavender?

Even in death they lie tucked up together.

Instructions for decoding an illness

> *Taught from infancy that beauty is woman's sceptre, the
> mind shapes itself to the body, and roaming round its gilt
> cage, only seeks to adorn its prison.*
> Mary Wollstonecraft

Migraine is a woman's attribute
a malady of impulses,
moral instinct in excess.
It's a cozy excuse
for shutting oneself off in quarantine.
Migraine is a glowworm
forcing its love on a mosquito
and at the very moment the passion
turns on it, lays light in the belly
like some dwindling essence.
Migraine is the business of poets
who impatiently swear off Babel.
It is the sickness of the stubborn:
the beautiful changing their skins
                    to turn adolescent.

They have migraines out of remorse.

Who can deny a migraine
smeared on like too much lipstick?
Like an exaggerated blush?

Greek goddesses
and Phoenician women
use a turban to hide its swelling up.
Lesbia was hit by a migraine of the heart.
Minerva had it in her skin.
We are the only ones to suffer migraines of the head.

My aunt recommends Pentateuch.
Layer by layer
destiny unfolds through these migraines
an astrological sign
a night patrol of memory
that scares away the appetite.

Migraine opens up a droning
                    an atrocious silence.
It's an excuse to re-examine history:
a nun was defrocked
for going in search of sedatives.
It turned up in paradise
and expanded to the ladies
who have ritual habits
and dye their hair purple.

It is a fiendish blessing, an outfit
by clever needleworkers
who stuck pins in the sceptre.

Migraine is what drives the wolf
down the road to restraint
into the mirage:
                    light.

Some of us

Gather to give each other courage.
Analyze every smell
sniff out rebellion
in the scent of a dissident.
Dream of the same barren plains.
Are fortune tellers. Smear imported powders
over vacant faces.
Cook passionately.

With the stubbornness of a planet
revolve around the same elements.
Go back to our rooms
beseiged.
Cover ourselves in satin.
To unseal their bodies apply makeup to our weariness.
In bed and on the operating room table
deliver ourselves with the same discipline.

Door in

At the third attempt
to get out
I saw the moon through the vagina.
My biological clock
runs no place:
I was born at night
and knew in that instant the hour of my death.
I have never written a poem in the morning.
I have roc birds
and carry owls sewn into my womb.
I must tell you:

when the moon is full it puts me in heat.
Where I come from, bats sing
till mockingbirds go deaf.
Those of us born at midnight
know our line:
the cemetery awaits us from childhood.
We visit our graves
and our epitaph
alludes to folk who,
running with wolves,
learnt to howl.

Door out

I wanted to know the exact time coitus woke me up out of death.
I was not consulted. They hung a necklace of bones about me to
distinguish me from others. Who was blowing into my ear?
Someone dug in their heels, tossing me into the tide. To make my
cycle complete, the undertow returned me to this world. It said,
Until the weariness sets in, suicides will be born, and vanished like a
ghost.

In transit

Today is Saturday. Saturday at the edge.
I'm speaking of another time
when ships were wrecked for the love of mermaids.

I have time until tomorrow.
A cloak, blown big by the air, covers me on my way.
I will linger there.

I don't regret the lack of light. Conjurations are, by nature,
nocturnal. I remember a fish tank: semi-circular,
far away; in my far-away house, the fish fry sleep.
In the same sweep the sea gathers up the bay, comes out
and out like the tourists to pore over the vault of heaven
decorated with stars. Venus is the sign of sailors,
of those who have lost their rudder in drink.

From your part of the world you watch me.
From sidereal space, the perspective is more accurate.
This is my young body; this—the scar that runs through me.
I am searching for my origins.
I come from a family of emigrants.

Rootlessness made me impatient before.
Am I able to toy with my surname?
Monstrous wings grow on my back.
I must live in the mud and the waste.
We have a passion for light in common.
I fall, seized by neon light.
Venus,
we love times past so much
that our nostalgia becomes a sort of adultery.
Mosconas by birth
from Bulgaria
arrived to drop me in a city
out of which I later do honour to the name. The slowest of
        twilights
comes closer. Ay, what do you do with this dizziness?

A woman like me moves out and away.
A ship founders on the high sea.
Look at me, spreading out under your sway.
The mantle of my wings is already hovering over Sunday.
I don't regret the lack of light, I told you,

even though my name demands it.
Drifting water lilies
flaunt new petals.
Twenty-seven years was time enough to die.

Venus herself
          hides in the dark.

Portrait of tortoise with woman

1

The glass goblet
features a fake pond of blue stones
                              and white sand.
On the bottom moves a tortoise.
While I dream
talk to me about your shell
the skeletons of live fish that feed me.

Talk to me with your parched palate and your inaccessible eyes.
Open up a shore
so the heat in my own plexus can escape.

Give back my snail shell
the lost sheen that is obscured on me.
Take a cloth
clean my glass house
that turns light in on the pond.

2

Its dreams change, facing the movement of waters.
Over the stones it climbs.
Not wanting to feel pushed by the river's inertia.

What thread sustains it in its passage?
Pay no attention to its longevity:
                        only what it augurs.

3

A mother braids her daughter's hair.
Dwells on the fine artifice of a house
beneath the hardness of her skin.
In her imagination she watches
a tightrope-walker tip over.
Sees a trapeze swing, its unguided movements.

Her empty house:
everything in the same spot,
not even the manias have moved.
The gasp that breathes life
into her internal motion
her cardinal points
has disrupted everything.

4

A woman is leaning over
into the venetian blinds, balancing
heavily on the broken wicker of a chair.
She watches the street impassively
remembers her aunt
dreads the epidemic of a common destiny.
A girl child is crying at her side;
she calms her by clapping her own eyes
on the dark eyes of the child.
She turns off the lights.
Sinks in under the sheets and waits
with equal obstinacy
to transform the skeleton
that has made her turn turtle.

Elegy

I lend you my mouth for you to speak.
I lend you my ears so you can hear
what your mouth says.

Tightrope-walker to the bone until the very end
don't you see how you keep us dangling?
What will we do with your clothes
your pyjamas
your pearl necklace?
What will we do with the piano?

I'm asking you to come back.
Today
marks one year since you left.
In the presence of the stone that covers you
beneath it
I'd like to be between earth and marble.

A year ago you quit sleeping
and for a year I've been dreaming you
princess of the depths.
Your glasses on the desk
lend light to no one else's eyes.

On the seventh storey
I sat on the floor
to be nearer the ground.
I lend you my mouth
my keen nerves.
I don't want the years you lived.
My twenty-two will do me.

I know you survived several wars
lost your children along the way

a bomb destroyed your house.
They took away your records
your favourite dress.

You carried on with no partner.
I was left fatherless
you dressed in black
and what good did it do?

What a circus you made of it
what a wet blanket
what a frill on you.
The roof suffocates you
this metal house
your hoarse voice haunting like the wind.
I want to tear up the roots that tie you
dig them in under the soles of my feet
give you my life.
Haul you off your swings, winded,
out of your weightless laugh.

Come back and say something to me.

On a daguerreotype

She speaks a Spanish learned post-war
cleans walls
hangs pictures
changes the tapestry on her rocking chair
she is setting the stage for her death

Her old age
flows like blood along a clotted artery

Her deaths
                    revived in picture frames from Istanbul
Gloomy likenesses

Photographs of a couple
in one another's arms in a garden near the sea
A girl
holding her daughter by the hand
The two of them dressed for the cold

It opens with a look in on her domestic animals
the image of herself she kept in her own memory, forgotten

Her patience
tightens like a string
shoots arrows that are not willingly let fly

Seated in the rocking chair
She stares straight at her dead husband
She cries the long-held sorrow of a lost family

Suicides buried face-down
The patriarchs dream their messianic dream

The cemetery is the border of this heart

For the void

A man and a woman are
for the void, light-lustre.

"Every man for himself and the devil take the hindmost,"
there was my father singing next to Robert Frost.

Then, off into the kitchen
to bring in the blood of the lamb.

No witch or gypsy he
was ever so simply dead.

Tiresias

If she should come with a branch of tamarind in her hand,
and between the leaves woo over my lover and I with her
        sweetness,
if we were to drink deep from her glass,
half-wedded, half-unknown,
if you, serpent Tiresias, should join
in and my sex unfold its fullness,
if my lover were to suckle the handsome concubine
and I squeeze the rice grains for the newlywed
between my thighs, tell me, Tiresias,
who would enjoy the trial more
of being the one cut into the better half?

The fling

I fling off this Persian wrap
and lotus petals
fly around the room.
I don't want to go over and over the thing.

Nonetheless, the fallen colours,
my naked,
shaking body,
remind me of the fling.

Stars spike
the dark of night with anís.
I watch myself melt into God's
void, and not into your arms.

Floating beings

> *How might a life be on the surface?*
> *Happy? And ought we to despise it for*
> *that? Perhaps there's a deal more to the surface,*
> *perhaps everything not on the surface is false.*
> Elías Canetti

For you, love, I propose to be a surface,
to be only a body in your eyes,
to be only a rhythm on your tongue,
to be the info on your Internet.

I propose, love, to be
your campfire for the night,
and like an orchid in April,
to lower the landing gear,

147

so that exactly the weight of your wings
keeps your pattern on hold
inside of my outside.

I am aware that flowers open
and I open too, less perfectly;
I lack, well, the divine simplicity
of only being an outside.

For you, love, I propose I be a surface,
I be a passing season,
return to a husbandry of paradise
with no high-tech trees of knowledge,

only orchids, give me orchids
(male and female of the flower).

I propose, love, I revert
to the very letter and love you
till depth us do part.

TRANSLATIONS BY KATE BRAID

FOR THE VOID, TIRESIAS, THE FLING, AND FLOATING
BEINGS TRANSLATED BY GEORGE McWHIRTER.

MYRIAM MOSCONA IS THE DAUGHTER OF SEPHARDIC PARENTS WHO CAME TO MEXICO FROM BULGARIA. SHE WAS BORN IN MEXICO CITY IN 1955. SHE HAS PUBLISHED THE FOLLOWING BOOKS OF POETRY: **ÚLTIMA JARDÍN** (EL TÚCAN DE VIRGINIA, 1983); **LAS VISITANTES** (JOAQUÍN MORTÍZ, 1989), WHICH WON THE AGUASCALIENTES NATIONAL POETRY PRIZE, A SHORT BOOK OF POETRY FOR CHILDREN, **LAS PREGUNTAS DE NATALIA** (CINTLI-CNCA, 1982); AND **EL ARBOL DE LOS NOMBRES** (GOVERNMENT FOR THE STATE OF JALISCO-CUATRO MENGUANTE, 1992). SHE ALSO PRODUCES A TELEVISION PROGRAM FOR CANAL 22 IN MEXICO CITY. HER **DE FRENTE Y DE PERFIL: SEMBLANZAS DE POETAS**, A BOOK OF PHOTOGRAPHS AND INTERVIEWS WITH MEXICAN POETS, APPEARED FROM CIUDAD DE MEXICO-DDF IN 1995. WITH THE COLLABORATION OF ADRIANA GONZÁLEZ MATEOS, SHE TRANSLATED A VOLUME OF WILLIAM CARLOS WILLIAMS' WORK INTO SPANISH, **LA MÚSICA DEL DESIERTO**, FOR WHICH SHE RECEIVED THE NATIONAL PRIZE FOR THE TRANSLATION OF POETRY IN 1996.

KATE BRAID IS A POET-CARPENTER, WHO WAS BORN IN CALGARY, ALBERTA, IN 1947. HER FIRST BOOK WAS **COVERING ROUGH GROUND** (POLESTAR PRESS, 1991), WHICH WON THE PAT LOWTHER AWARD FOR POETRY FROM THE LEAGUE OF CANADIAN POETS; **TO THIS CEDAR FOUNTAIN** (POLESTAR, 1995), HER SECOND BOOK, WAS NOMINATED FOR THE DOROTHY LIVESAY PRIZE AT THE BC BOOK AWARDS. HER LATEST, **INWARD TO THE BONES: GEORGIA O'KEEFFE'S JOURNEY WITH EMILY CARR**, WAS PUBLISHED BY POLESTAR IN THE SPRING OF 1998. SHE HAS JUST COMPLETED HER MASTER OF FINE ARTS AT UBC AND HAS TAUGHT THE SENIOR YEAR POETRY WORKSHOP THERE. SHE LIVES IN BURNABY, BC, WITH HER LAWYER HUSBAND, JOHN.

VERÓNICA VOLKOW (1955 -)

The washerwoman

Her hands feel rough to her, like fish
blind fish that thrash against the rock
incessantly against the rock over years and years;
she looks at the night pierced with eyes
damp shifting looks, slippery faces, mute, that are lost
the looks of girls with shiny faces
the blighted looks of tired mothers.
The day ends and the people return to their houses
and water pours, droning from the tap like a song
the water has lost the shape of the pipes
has forgotten its memory of the riverbed on the mountain
and has made its way
lined about by its obstacles
like feet, like eyes, like hands.
She looks at the shadows that people drag
shadows on the walls, the corners, the streets
passing stains that mark the roads
laborious despairing roads
that look only, perhaps, for some permanence.

The adolescent

Is extreme beauty prohibitive?
Are you prohibitive?
Your youth displayed in all its impudence
like a grotesque tiger
oblivious and lawless?
                    In your body
child and adult have not been joined
like the sea and stone, indissoluble and alien.
And the shadows of down and sensuality
are parasitic orchids in your childish smile.
What rudeness!
How implacable the blind pride!
How tempting only to see the glitter,
though it is a trick of the moment,
the sharp caress of contempt.
But your hands are made of strength and invisible
impotence
and a secret sentence that time readies
to level us all.
How dark beauty is towards itself!
How dark the death that little by little subdues it!

We can choose this or whichever other path
and all are dispersed or end up painted on a wall,
there are afternoons in which the hallways dry up
and things look like pulpless shells
and mothers die of forgetfulness and their weaving
without thread.
There are afternoons in which shoes yawn in the shade
under beds
and toads lie dead beneath the pavement,
there are afternoons in which one can hear the hollows

in the bells
and be the mute clapper of a body in a day
that dissipates,
it's like becoming little   so little
as to lose yourself in the surrounding atoms.
There are afternoons in which it is the same to go forward or
            stay,
the same to be a man or a woman.
a crumbling wall, or the dog that urinates on it,
an old woman that sings with rotting teeth
or a mirror standing in a hotel room,
and you can climb the stairs, open all the doors,
and find the forbidden flesh that glows
on the horizon of the bed like a cloud.

Cabaret

The music pulls us,
the dance circles and advances
like a dense and dirty river between the tables,
alcoholic eyes, hands,
breasts, arms,
spike heels, satin waists;
and we all dance without looking,
thirsty tongues in the well of a kiss,
dirty glasses, unlit butts,
toothless awnings.
Only the skin gleams
in the mirror of fingers.

We might appear

We might appear, at times, to be a shadow
that licks tirelessly at a body,
the echo diluting the shout,
the fire that greens the wood again.
We might appear to be the clandestine granny
who touches the breasts of her granddaughter
with a guilty, jealous gesture.
We might appear to be the eternally exiled from the skin
of transluscent beasts
or the ancestral ship that lists
in the confines of the waves.
It is enough to look at the back end of our road:
a walled-in sea that doesn't open,
frozen beasts that can't look out for themselves
and further back   further away
                —paralyzed turquoise—
the gentle waves   the breeze.
If I could at least hold on to you,
if I could at least remember,
if only even outside in dreams
the walls would open,
if they would open.

A notion

The present
is only the brilliance of light on these rocks,
the yellow house that remains,
the pines aligned
that hum in the wind
like a vast and monotonous harp.
Just the chairs here, the tables, the glasses left behind,
the axes of ancient movements.
Invisible hues of laughter and the longing
of love, of crime,
in the quickening or slowing down of footsteps
or in the rub of a hand on wood,
actions very little different
from the fall of leaves or rain.
Stones that slowly wear thin,
papers that yellow,
walls that cave in,
as if this were the only script to history,
flameless glow of the blackened wick,
indecipherable lives in the contours of the bones.
The visible, final horizon of seeing.
And if
the shadow moves
with which memory traces another instant over the instant,
the notion embedded in layers of rock and wood,
it's the ultimate transparency of time.

Untitled

I can't say that word any more
but I can kiss the broadness of your back
with the everyday air that marks a habit,
with the motion of a plant
that seizes the earth,
of the wheel turning,
of things that simply
are there.
I can't say that word any more,
nor ask,
nor long for it,
and like the eternal tedium of the hills for the bull
my body stretches on and on in your pupils.
I can't tell any more,
I can't tell if we might have lost the word,
but things are happening in slow rivers of light
like at the dawn of some timid animal.

Landscape from an automobile

Blue is the colour of distance,
the colour in which mountains are lost,
sunk into the sky.
It is the colour that brings puddles closer,
out of the unreachable deep of distance.
Between the meticulous grasses and rocks,
swallows that open
and close like fists
are photographed by the water for an instant
and revert to shadow over the ground.

There, with lines of trees,
furrows of earth,
men work the pattern of the countryside
into the distance,
the symmetry to their design dotted
like the rocks over the irregular hills.

River

The river is only a glimmer among the rocks
that falls   falls
the constant boom of a lyric
like the rustle in grass
that never ceases.
Trees do a flawless
dance with the wind
move with
the jerk of gears, shifting.
Wind
the wind rises
murmurs   slurs, becomes more wind.
The lake in the afternoon changes
its facets like a mirror
from sunny
to metallic.
The lake is blue now
and gradually like the neighbouring air
transparent   along the edges.
In the mist water is stone
mist covers the wood like a bottomless shroud
open to pass through anywhere.

Beginning

I

Hunger is the body's first eye
the first eye in the night of the body
the eye that flesh watches flesh with   for the first time

and a bloody darkness is tangled inside
                     the eye
my feet   my teeth
                     my fingers see through you

                     the eye
I watch you with   as though down the centuries,
in the night of touch
                         that night
so like the night of the fish
             the tiger
             the serpent
so like life's first night

We are beasts again once we shut our eyes
and our bodies are clamped like jaws
                welded to the taste of these shapes

II

Only on the skin does there exist
             this thin atmosphere
between visceral night
             and the other night
which is perhaps the same
that is kindled in the stars
             or lightning
the same night that scratches at itself

In the dark I touch your night lips
                    your night teeth
                    your night tongue
in the darkness my fingers follow
your arms   your shoulders
my blind, deaf fingers
that don't see   or hear you
                    configure you

skin   great eyelid
shapes bestowing only footprints
                              shadow faces
like a language of identical sounds
that tells our skin of the world
hands that move like hushed mouths
like starving gullets filled with broken cries
a movement of lips where the voice has been lost
the skin   the raw throat   the ear
untangled labyrinth from which invisible music escapes
from which your shapeless words escape like breath
from which the sparkle in your eyes escapes
the colour of your hair your far-off face

caresses that imprint shadow glyphs on skin
faint pachyderm fingers
gliding shark's tongue
oyster teeth
Are they the ruins of ancient statues in bare flesh
or beings that are round pitchers
        precious herds bunched
on the plains of silent skin?

III

But in the labyrinth of our hearing
the voice runs

your voice, which is a magic sea in my ear
oceans of things already sounding

In your voice I hear my name
the names of countless cities
the story of a life you are telling me
I hear a phrase you say very slowly
words I can repeat to myself like a song
      —the shape of time lasting the same—
words that bring your voice freshly minted
your teeth   your body
     like a secret bas relief
     that sounds
your presence on the earth
         a volume
far beyond voice   unpronounceable

IV

And if I were made of skin to the bottom of me
a deep-skinned animal
         a statue
a maze outside like that within

and if I were skin
inexhaustible as sand
         as cloud
on which wind stamps its invisible face
infinite spiral with a ceaseless face
all skin like a mirror
         which your body
would funnel into shapes and colours
like air   a melody on a flute already
a river that is the liquid sculpture of its flow
an eye that becomes a sculpture

your hands   your mouth   your
      touching me

V

lovers
only have hands to love with
                have only their hands
hands that are winged feet over the body
hands that hunt tirelessly
the shivering animal with sunken eyes
fingers that are firewood when bodies burn
are branches on which caresses flower
flowers that are birds of the air are flames are hands
hands lost in the scrawl of light

hands roaming over the skin on the body
like star-fingers waking to the touch
like newborn suns   like shooting star-gems
secret gods that trace the shapes of night

VI

I look at your shadow
I look at your shadow that falls over my hands
like black rain onto my palms
night rain
              your night
the night at your back
your double that you drag
like a murdered Hector

the ink your body writes in
Your picture in my hands
the wreck of yourself that shreds
the colour from the shapes
the tongue in your feet that repeats your

death to you
which has toppled your body
just a moment ago
the design   the host   the word
a sliver of you in the teeth of my hands

VII

Our bodies jammed together like mirrors
jammed together like mirrors by desire
my eyes lost
in the well of yours
Your eyes suspended
                    in mine
                    towards an infinity
an identical series
a way to the same worlds   a smaller
                              view
of what is eternal recapitulated

your voice works your breath
                              your voice
sudden blaze in the silence
a visible shadow of sound
                    from the past to the present
                    from the present to the future
words spent again and again, like echoes   like coins
heraldically cradled in the cavern of the mouth

          I close my eyes
your heart is your blood wave
your fingers shimmering fishes
your teeth   the iceberg of the skeleton
                    we join
in a wet kiss inside
an enormous kiss   an inside sea

we know the certainty of pleasure only
that light buried
in the dark will of our bodies.

VIII

deepest darkness
that bares the skies
and reaches its fingers to the stars
profound darkness
in which in the distance
the simplicity of fire burns
distant worlds open
                their secret taps
and forms are the sources
of elemental springs
the light sings on the river
and from throat of water into quietness

                        a mine of distant flames
the night also goes right to your depths
the bodies
the secret mineral in your bodies
is transformed
with the simplcity of water
in the darkness of the mouth
or a star's sudden appearance in your hands
from far away
with a caress from nothing at all
            from where
did man carve the first fire?

IX

next to your body my body is the footstep your body
it is the eye   the ear to your body
            I hear your arms
                    your teeth

                your tongue
                your legs
with all my whole skin I listen to the shape of your body

next to your body my body
is your body in another form
like water that is incandescent ice
or the spigot of fire in things
                your body
roars into mine
                and you are a cleft call
                a stellar call
a mute call   of flesh   in my body
tell me   is not fire
the seed of distant worlds
the strange and sudden shape of its nearness?

X

you're naked
            your smoothness is endless
you tremble in my fingers
your breathing flutters in your body
                you are
like a bird in my hands
                    vulnerable
as only desire could make you vulnerable
such smooth pain with which we are touching
that giving in which we share
the abandonment of victims

pleasure like a jaw
devours us

Tropic

The tropical
is a lacework of immediacies
everywhere bursts of wind
set flowers off
like small suns and everything
out of small spigots comes flushing
the rainbow is a harp of light
a thing of air
light lives in a flash of gems through the sky
everything is a mirror
and in every mirror the day dances
night is the stone on the eye
a stone that has grown into light
light that bursts into music
in bursts of the random
life burns
only in that freedom can I be real
my root is in the multiple.

TRANSLATIONS BY IONA WHISHAW

VERÓNICA VOLKOW WAS BORN IN MEXICO CITY IN 1955. UNTIL THE AGE OF EIGHTEEN SHE LIVED IN THE HOUSE OF HER GREAT–GRANDFATHER, LEON TROTSKY, IN COYOACÁN, MEXICO CITY. SHE STUDIED HISPANIC LITERATURE AT COLUMBIA UNIVERSITY IN NEW YORK CITY. HER BOOKS OF POETRY ARE **LA SIBILA DE CUMAS** (MARTÍN PESCADOR, MEXICO, 1974), **LITORAL DE TINTA** (CUADERNOS DE POESÍA, UNAM, MEXICO CITY, 1979), AND **EL INICIO** (EDICIONES FRANCISCO TOLEDO, JUCHITÁN, 1983), AND **CAMINOS/WAYS** (EDICIONES TOLEDO, MEXICO CITY, 1989). SHE IS A RESPECTED TRANSLATOR AND HAS PUBLISHED BOOKS OF VICTOR SERGE, JOHN ASHBERY, ELIZABETH BISHOP AND MICHAEL HAMBURGER IN SPANISH TRANSLATION. A PROSE BOOK, **DIARIO DE ÁFRICA** WAS PUBLISHED BY SIGLO VENTÍUNO EDITORES IN 1988.

IONA WHISHAW'S FAMILIARITY WITH SPANISH DEVELOPED FROM PERIODS OF TIME SPENT IN LATIN AMERICA, WHERE HER FATHER TRAVELLED AS A GEOLOGIST. HER TRANSLATIONS OF VERÓNICA VOLKOW HAVE APPEARED IN *TRI-QUARTERLY, THE XAVIER REVIEW, THE LITERARY REVIEW, VISIONS INTERNATIONAL* AND CITY LIGHT'S ANTHOLOGY OF MEXICAN POETRY EDITED BY JUVENAL ACOSTA: **LIGHT FROM A NEARBY WINDOW**. SHE TEACHES SCHOOL IN VANCOUVER.

George McWhirter

George McWhirter was born in Belfast, Northern Ireland, in 1939. He was educated at Queen's University Belfast and came to Canada in 1966 after living in Barcelona, Spain. His first book, **Catalan Poems** (Oberon Press, 1971), shared the 1972 Commonwealth Poetry Prize with Chinua Achebe's **Cry, Soul Brother.** His translations and editing of **The Selected Poems of José Emilio Pacheco** won the 1987 F.R. Scott Prize for translation from the League of Canadian Poets and F.R. Scott Foundation. His novel, **Cage,** which is set in the towns of Tetelcingo and Cuautla in Mexico, won the 1987 Ethel Wilson Prize for Fiction at the BC Book Awards. He has been working at his translations of José Emilio Pacheco, Homero Aridjis and Gabriel Zaid for the past two decades. In the Department of Theatre, Film & Creative Writing at the University of British Columbia, where he has taught in the Creative Writing Program and been involved with **PRISM** *international* as Poetry Editor, Editor, and Advisory Editor for Translations since 1970, he leads the Literary Translation group.